# Blessed
## by an Angel

Publications International, Ltd.

**Contributing writers:** Jane Edwards Aldrich: 275; Joanne Bailey Baxter: 227; Dianne Benton: 93; Patti Bicrcr: 268; Lori Bledsoe: 25; Corrie ten Boom, as told to Muriel Larson: 160; Renie Szilak Burghardt: 106; Cecil Burnette: 132; Mary Chandler: 8; Linda Chiara: 53; Jackie Clements-Marenda: 328; Louise Coffman: 113; Phil Contino: 74; Elaine Coringrato: 357; Katherine Erwin: 203; Susan Fahncke: 190, 352; Pat Gilbers: 308; Jennifer Greco: 262; Judie Gulley: 39, 294; Carole Hall: 339; Bonnie Compton Hanson: 16, 270; Margaret Anne Huffman: 118; Ellen Javernick: 139, 168, 246, 257; Marie Jones: 19, 68, 211, 320, 346; La'Kisha DeVon Jordan: 378; Karen Leet: 4, 179, 185, 240; Trista Linman: 230; Mary Maxey: 126; Brandy Morris: 365; Robbie Morris, as told to Frances E. Sames: 100; Barbara Morrow: 300; Kathleen Muldoon: 222; Deby Murray: 148; Ellen Pill: 303, 371; Janet Rodda: 154; Ann Russell: 45; Susan Sage: 218; Elsie Stover Schad: 122; Ernest Shubird: 174, 252; Nanette Snipes: 60, 335; Carol Solstad: 80; Barbara Spotts: 314; Carol Stigger: 31; Irma W. Taylor: 88; LeAnn Thieman: 207; Shirley Valencia: 284; Elizabeth White: 279; Lynne Zielinski: 198.

**Illustrator:** Mary O'Keefe Young

**Acknowledgments:**
Unless otherwise noted, all scripture quotations are taken from the *New Revised Standard Version* of the Bible, copyright ©1989, by the Division of Christian Education of the National Council of the Churches of Christ in the United States of America. Used by permission. All rights reserved.

Scripture quotations marked (KJV) are taken from *The Holy Bible, King James Version*. Copyright © 1977, 1984, Thomas Nelson Inc., Publishers.

Scripture quotations marked (NIV) are taken from *The Holy Bible, New International Version*. Copyright © 1973, 1978, 1984 International Bible Society. Used by permission of Zondervan Publishing House. All rights reserved.

ISBN-13: 978-1-4127-1374-0
ISBN-10: 1-4127-1374-9

Manufactured in China

8 7 6 5 4 3 2 1

Library of Congress Control Number: 2006903678

# Contents

# Angel Wings

ANGELS GUARD US, guide us, watch over us, and bring us comfort, courage, and hope. They are God's messengers, reaching out to us to remind us of his love and concern for us.

Throughout recorded history, angels appear again and again in the crucial moments of people's lives. In the Bible, an angel spoke to Mary. Other angels sang at the birth of Jesus, God's Son. Another angel warned Joseph to flee with his family into Egypt for safety. And angels stood watch over the empty Easter tomb.

In our lives, angels are as close as others' outstretched hands. They reach for us with hands of support, patting our shoulders in encouragement, tending us in illness and darkest despair, and holding our hands when we are afraid.

We recognize God's message to us through his ministering angels: We are not alone! God cares. He always has and always will. Perhaps that's why angels fascinate us and why we watch angel movies and television shows, read angel books, wear angel jewelry, and collect angel figurines. Most of us hear stories from friends and family—amazing tales of angels intervening to protect or guide. With every angel story, we feel anew the awe and wonder of their presence, the sense of security that they're close by and watching over us, and above all else, the promise that God cares enough to send them.

We decorate Christmas trees with angels, listen eagerly to angel stories, and hold in the secret places of our hearts the expectation that angels hover nearby. At any moment, they might appear as a loved one, a stranger, or another of God's creatures when we need them most. And when they do, they touch us, and we are forever changed, for they have become a real presence in our lives.

So, step into the pages of this book, experience the joy and security of knowing that these angelic messengers are part of our lives, share the comfort and hope they bring, and draw strength and peace knowing angels come to us because God loves us. Read and enjoy these inspiring stories. Keep this lovely collection on your bedside table or in your briefcase. Give a copy to a friend as a reminder of God's constant, protective presence. Reread and treasure this beautiful book. And listen carefully as you read—you may hear angel wings beating gently upon your heart!

# Angels of Mercy

The angel of the Lord said to her, "...the Lord has given heed to your affliction."

Genesis 16:11

*angel* *Lord* *affliction*

# The Good Physician

EARING A WHITE medical coat with his name on the pocket, Dr. Ronald Greene, a stocky man who looked to be in his sixties, greeted me in his Chicago office on a warm June day in 1958. A fringe of white hair framed his head. He wore glasses—and a huge smile.

"Your first baby?" he asked.

"Yes."

"Sit down, please, and tell me about yourself." He sat at his desk, his bright eyes looking into mine.

I explained that I worked as a secretary and that my husband and I had moved to Chicago so he could attend Northwestern Dental School in the fall. Dr. Greene glanced at the patient information chart I had filled out. "You live on Kenmore. That's near Wrigley Field, isn't it?"

I nodded.

"I love watching the Cubs. Have you been to Wrigley Field?"

I shook my head. "Not yet."

He chuckled. "That's one place struggling students can go on the cheap." He sighed. "I think back to when I was in med school more years back than I care to remember. Learned to live on a shoestring." He paused. "Tuition has skyrocketed since my day. How do you manage?"

"Until school starts, Don's working days as a chemist at Industrial Adhesives and nights at Banker's Life & Casualty. I work for Blue Shield."

As I talked, Dr. Greene made notes on my chart.

"No relatives in the area?"

I shook my head. "No."

"Home phone?"

"Not yet, but we'll be getting a phone in a couple of months. We can be reached at the work numbers."

"Well, young lady," he said, "my nurse will give you a gown for the exam, and then we'll talk about what to expect during your pregnancy. I'll answer any questions you might have. All right?"

I hesitated for just a moment. Dr. Greene must have sensed what I needed to know. "You have Blue Shield, right?"

I nodded. "It's an 80/20 plan."

"Good. I'm charging half my usual fee," he said. "Whatever your insurance pays will cover everything."

Tears gathered in my eyes. I knew that Dr. Greene had a reputation for being one of the best obstetricians in Chicago and was widely respected as a researcher and as a doctor. "That doesn't sound like enough, Dr. Greene."

He winked and grinned. "Help someone else when you can," he said. "Besides, I love bringing babies into the world."

Neither of us counted on complications.

I kept each appointment faithfully. The nausea disappeared in a few weeks, and except for being exhausted some days after work, I felt wonderful. I wrote weekly letters to my mother and mother-in-law, sharing my excitement and my joy. How I wished that my mother lived in Chicago instead of in Utah! Still, I made friends in the community and in the church, some of whom were also expectant moms.

Knowing our financial situation, and with tuition coming due soon, my boss said I could work until the middle of January—one month before my due date.

On a freezing January day after work, I crossed the long bridge to the bus stop. The icy wind from Lake Michigan ate through my coat and gloves, chilling me to the bone. I waited, shivering, hoping the bus would be on time.

As the bus rounded the corner and then stopped, I stepped off the curb to board. A man raced in front of me, shoved me out of his way, and bounded onto the bus. I lay in a heap, facedown, in the cold, gray slush.

Another passenger helped me up. "Are you all right?" he asked.

"I think so." Tears stung my eyes. My scraped cheeks felt like bits of gravel were embedded in them. Sleet clung to my hair and dripped onto my face. I felt my ankle swelling. But I wasn't crying because of my injuries. I was scared that the fall had hurt my baby. I eased my way into the crowded bus. The man who had pushed me buried his face in his newspaper as I passed. A young boy, about 12, gave me his seat.

Resting my hands on my stomach, I closed my eyes and prayed silently for what seemed like an eternity, waiting. Finally, the baby moved and was kicking as it always did this time of night.

The next afternoon I saw Dr. Greene. Like a loving father, he wrapped his arms around me, comforting me and assuring

me that babies are well protected inside the womb. His exam showed no cause for concern.

A month later, I saw Dr. Greene again. "The baby hasn't dropped yet," he said. "You have another week to ten days before delivery."

My baby had other plans. Riding home in our car with my husband's carpool buddies, my water broke. "I think we'd better hurry home," I said. "We need to call Dr. Greene and get back to the hospital."

An intern met us at the door. "The doctor needs X-rays," he said, rushing me down the hall. "He's on his way."

Thirty minutes later Dr. Greene arrived. I had no labor pains. Not one.

"Your baby's head is pinching the umbilical cord," he said. "The greenish-brown amniotic fluid is a signal that the baby is in distress. I need to do an emergency C-section—now!"

My back burned when the anesthesiologist gave me a spinal, but during the surgery I felt only pressure. No pain. I heard voices while Dr. Greene delivered the baby and worked to get him to breathe. I waited. My heart all but stopped. Silence. Then, a baby's cry!

"It's a beautiful boy!" Dr. Greene said in a choked voice, holding Michael close so I could see him. Tears glistened in his eyes. "That was a close call."

Dr. Greene insisted on a ten-day hospital stay. He knew I would be on my own once I left the hospital, since Don was in school and holding down two jobs. He ordered me not to climb the steep stairs to our second-story apartment for two weeks—after Don helped me the first time—and to keep in touch by phone. I followed his instructions implicitly.

A month later I was back in Dr. Greene's office with Michael for my final checkup. "Dr. Greene," I said, opening my purse, "I know you hadn't counted on a C-section when you quoted me your price for delivering the baby. Don and I want..."

He closed my purse and took my hand in his. "Remember what I told you on your first visit?" he asked. "Life isn't about money—it's about helping others. Do that, and I will have been repaid many times over." He smiled that gentle smile. "Promise?"

"Yes, I promise."

Many years have passed since I made that promise back in 1958, and Dr. Ronald Greene has long since left us. Yet, each time I anonymously give a scholarship, pick up a restaurant tab for an elderly couple, slip a $20 bill into the hand of a stranger in need, or share my time, encouragement, and love with someone struggling along life's road, I think about my promise and see a kindly doctor smiling down from the heavens.

*The Eternal Father has blessed us with his hosts of angels to come to our aid and lead us out of the wilderness of fear, doubt, and confusion.*

# Dorothy's Angelic Chauffeur

DOROTHY PERCHES ON the edge of the porch bench, feet gently tapping on the terra-cotta bricks of the patio as she waits patiently for her ride. It's Tuesday, and a new delivery of fresh peaches should be at her favorite farmstand. Thank goodness! With the church bake sale coming up in just a couple days, Dorothy had started to worry that she wouldn't be able to bake her renowned peach pie as she had done for more years than she cared to remember.

She sighs. Until she failed her driving test last year—at the age of 85!—she hadn't realized how dependent she was on her car. She used it to run errands, visit friends, and especially to drive across town to the movie theater. Dorothy tries to remember the last time she'd been to a movie. She used to see almost every new release, but now it's been a while since she's seen any movie at all. When she lost her license, she lost more than the ability to drive. She also lost her independence—her freedom. She still has the energy and the desire to bake pies, go to the movies, and socialize with her friends, but she no longer has the means to do these things.

She sighs again, then begins to smile as she sees a familiar van pull around the corner and turn into her driveway. Anne waves and grins from behind the wheel. "Come on," she calls. "The movie starts in an hour, and Sean Connery's not going to wait around for you forever!"

Dorothy gathers her purse, straightens her hat, and starts down the steps, grinning.

When Dorothy first met Anne through her church, she took an immediate liking to the energetic, friendly young woman. As their friendship developed, Dorothy began to recognize that Anne, who had never known her own grandparents, delighted in "adopting" surrogate grandparents. That was just fine with Dorothy, who already felt a strong tie to Anne.

When Anne saw Dorothy's despondence over losing her license, Anne got an idea. In no time, it seemed, she went to school and obtained a license permitting her to drive vans and even buses. Anne now uses this license to give joy to senior citizens, Dorothy included. Anne cheerfully chauffeurs her friends around on errands, but she also racks her brain to plan fun, worthwhile activities for them to enjoy. Some of their favorite excursions have been to the local zoo, a doll museum, the beach, and the glorious flower fields at the Botanic Gardens.

As Dorothy carefully steps into the van, ready for their outing—first to see the latest summer blockbuster and then on to the farmstand to take care of business—she reflects that Anne has been much more than a chauffeur for her. She is also her friend and her angel.

*Your special angel is always there,*
*To cheer, to comfort, to guide, to care.*

# The Moose

NEW HOUSE. New town. New school.

For a sixth grader, nothing could be more horrifying, especially if that sixth grader was Jared Cameron. Jared was small for his age, and he wore braces and glasses. Goodness, he might as well have put a sign on his forehead that said, "Total Nerd," because that's just how he felt walking through the doors of Granden Middle School.

Before the day was out, Jared found himself hating his new situation even more. Not one person talked to him, not even the other nerds. Little did Jared know that the worst was yet to come. When he walked into his final class, he found the only empty seat was next to a big, mean-looking boy, who glared at him with wolflike eyes. "Hey, nerd, have a seat," the boy said menacingly. Jared sat down, but not before the older boy managed to stick a wad of chewed gum on the chair. Jared closed his eyes in quiet despair, not even bothering to get up to remove the gum.

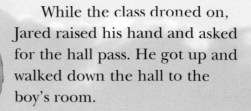

While the class droned on, Jared raised his hand and asked for the hall pass. He got up and walked down the hall to the boy's room.

Jared sensed his presence before he heard his voice. "Hey brace-face, you're gonna cause a car crash with all that glare!" Jared cringed, hoping the booming voice of the older boy was not intended for him. "Hey, four-eyes, you're gonna blind somebody with those Coke bottles!"

Jared ran into the boy's room, leaning on the door and catching his breath. He hoped a teacher would hear the commotion and come to his rescue, but no teacher came at that moment.

"Hey, little girl. Oh, sorry, I thought you were a girl, you're so small!" Now the voice was closer, just right outside the door, and it sounded even deeper and more menacing then before. Terrified, Jared planted his feet solidly and leaned hard against the door. He began to cry, an absolute no-no when dealing with a bully, but he couldn't help it.

That's when he heard the teacher's voice yelling at "Billy"—the bully in question—to get back to class.

Jared stayed in the bathroom for ten minutes, just to be safe, but he was even more frightened to find he was not alone when he heard a toilet flush. A much older and bigger boy, even bigger than Billy the Bully, emerged from the stall, washed his hands, and walked right by Jared and out the door without a word.

Jared held his breath and then went back to class. He dared not look at Billy, although he checked his chair before he sat down to make sure it was gum-free. When the bell rang, Jared tore from the room, determined to run the whole five blocks home and beg his parents to move back to their old neighborhood.

He was only two blocks away from home when he heard that voice again, taunting him. "Hey freaky deaky girly-boy! Think you can get away from me, do ya? Hey, girly-boy, freaky-face, idiot from outer space!"

Jared quickened his pace, but Billy's booming, teasing voice seemed even closer. Tears rolled down Jared's cheeks while he wiped at his runny nose with his sleeve.

One last corner to turn, and he would be on his street. Jared was running, but he could hear the sound of someone much larger coming up behind him, and then he felt the hand on his shoulder, pushing him down to the ground. Just before he closed his eyes, he noticed that Billy had brought along a crowd of onlookers eager to see a good nerd-beating. Jared thought about screaming, but sheer terror and the expectancy of a good whoopin' had rendered him speechless.

He closed his eyes and resigned himself to the first punch.

Jared heard the punch long before he felt it. In fact, he never felt it. When he dared open his eyes, amidst the yells and hollers of the onlookers, he noticed that Billy was down on the ground alongside him, nursing a sore cheek.

Standing over Billy was a hulk of a boy in blue jeans and a black jacket, glaring down at Billy with arms folded and chest puffed out. Jared had never seen such a big kid, but then he realized he had seen him in the boy's room earlier that day.

"You wanna fight some-body, fight me," the big kid growled, staring down at a cowering Billy, "and leave my friend here alone. You got that?"

Billy nodded dumbly, still rubbing his reddening cheek. Jared just sat there with his mouth open. DID HE SAY "FRIEND"?

The big kid held out his hand. "Name's The Moose." Jared reluctantly took his hand, and The Moose yanked the boy to his feet with a smile. "At your service."

Jared managed to squeak out his name, and they shook hands. As Billy got to his feet, The Moose put a protective arm around Jared. Billy looked at Jared with new respect, then he got the hint and ran away.

The Moose walked Jared to his house, but when Jared asked him to come in, he declined and said he had to move on.

That night, Jared excitedly told his parents all about his first day at school, about his almost-fight and a guy named The Moose, who came to his rescue. For the next few days, he looked for The Moose everywhere, but he couldn't find him. No one else ever seemed to know where he was either, including Billy, who had become Jared's new friend.

*When we suffer, angels wrap their wings around us*
*to comfort and protect us and give us time to heal.*
*When we are stronger, angels unfold their wings and*
*set us free to experience life again.*

# Family in Distress

I LOOKED AROUND TEARFULLY at the small, roach-infested apartment. It wasn't much, but it had been home for my two young daughters and me for the last couple months. Once again, we were being evicted for not paying rent, and I had only one more day to figure out where we could move. I didn't have any money or a job, and getting a job was difficult without a phone or a permanent address.

The doorbell rang, and I opened the door to find Monica standing on the steps. I'd met her around the neighborhood, and a sort of friendship was beginning to form. Monica was a dancer at a club a few blocks away; at night she transformed into "Monique."

"What's up?" Monica asked, glancing at the boxes piled everywhere.

"The girls and I have to move," I answered with an obvious sigh.

"Where to?" Monica asked in surprise.

25

"I have no idea. I don't have the money for deposits or anything this time. I think we're going to have to live in the car for a while." I forced back tears. It seemed so unfair to be putting my daughters through this again.

Monica moved a box off an ugly, worn-out chair and flopped down to put her feet up on the scratched coffee table. "Why don't you get a job at the club? With that red hair and those big green eyes, you'd be a real hit. The money's great! You'd make at least 100 to 200 bucks a night."

I shook my head. "I wouldn't have the guts to dance around like that."

"You get used to it," Monica assured me. "And you'd have enough money to move into a place after a few nights. Sure beats living in a car."

"Yeah, maybe," I replied.

Monica left, and I thought about her offer. The money sounded really tempting, especially with so few options in sight. But what would I tell my girls?

Things had been really tough for me since I divorced my husband and moved to the city. I had stood in line for free groceries quite a few times, and the girls and I had slept in our car and stayed in cheap motels more than once. Even so, was I desperate enough to become a dancer at Monica's club?

Dropping my head to my hands, I prayed, "Lord, I don't know what to do. I don't have anywhere to go, and I barely have enough food left to feed the girls for the next few days. What should I do, God? Should I take Monica's advice? Please help us, Lord. Help me understand your will."

Just as I finished my prayer, the girls came running through the door with one of their friends. "Mommy! Mommy! Can Jenny spend the night with us? Please? Please?" All three were bouncing up and down with excitement, and I thought wearily that I didn't have the energy to pack and keep up with all three of them that night.

"Oh, girls, you know I have to pack tonight. We're moving tomorrow, and I don't think it's a very good time to have company."

"But we'll be good. We promise! And we'll even help you pack." Three pairs of sweet little eyes pleaded with me, and, as usual, I couldn't resist.

"Oh, all right," I consented. "But you'd better make sure it's OK with Jenny's mom first." The girls screamed with delight as they headed out to Jenny's home nearby. Soon they were back with Jenny's mom, Renae.

"Hi, Renae," I said. "Sorry about the mess. We're getting ready to move and . . ." my voice trailed off in embarrassment.

"Don't worry about it," Renae replied cheerfully. "It looks better than my house on a good day," she laughed. "Where are you moving?"

"I don't know yet," I had to admit. "We have to be out of here tomorrow, though."

"Are you sure you want Jenny to stay over? It looks as if you have your hands full as it is. I would have them all stay with me, but I have to work tomorrow, and my mom is sick, and she doesn't like a lot of noise."

"Oh, sure, it's OK. She'll keep the girls occupied and out of my hair. I've got to figure something out between now and tomorrow at 3:00."

Renae, understanding my financial situation, made a gracious offer: "Why don't you stay in my apartment until you get on your feet? We're staying with my mom because she's too sick to stay by herself right now. And I really don't like the idea that  my apartment is sitting over there empty all the time. You never know when someone's going to figure it out and break in. It's small—only one bedroom—but you could store all your stuff in the garage until you get a place of your own. And, if you're interested, I know they're looking for people to work at the day-care center where Jenny goes in the afternoon. You could take your girls along with you."

I stared at her in disbelief. "Are you sure?" I stammered. "I don't know how long it would be before I could pay you back." I thought Renae must surely be an angel sent by God.

"You won't owe me anything," Renae said. "You'll be doing me a favor by keeping the thieves away from my door. If you'd like, you can borrow my old pickup to move your stuff."

After Renae left and the girls went out to play, I sank to my knees. "Thank you, Lord, for answering my prayers. I know you will always take care of me, and I should rely on you when I'm feeling desperate. I'm sorry I ever had any doubts." A peace came over me that I hadn't felt in a long time, and I returned to my packing with a much lighter heart.

*If ever you feel your arms are too short*
*to reach for the heavens, fear not,*
*for there will always be an angel reaching*
*out to meet you halfway.*

# Mary's Kids

MARY GONZALES LIVES one of life's greatest lessons: to love people and use things, rather than to use people and love things. Her message is unwritten, unspoken, and unmistakable. Her "things" do not include a bed or a reliable refrigerator. Mary and her husband sleep on spring sofas with tattered upholstery. When their old refrigerator groans and shudders to a stop, she shrugs and says, "It always turns itself back on in a few days." Home repairs are beyond her budget; her broken door and peeling linoleum match her neighbors' homes, as does her bedraggled yard. In this derelict neighborhood on the south side of Chicago, few flowers bloom and little grass grows. People who love things must turn to theft and drug dealing to buy them. And many of them do.

But not "Mary's Kids," the neighborhood children who are touched by her love.

Mary's love is tough at times, tender at other times, and always vast and unshakable. She is the involved parent, the birthday cake baker, the party planner, and the stay-at-home mom for neighborhood children who do not get enough love and attention in their own homes. Mary meets the kids bursting out of school who crowd around her waving their report cards. She smiles and hugs the good students. She frowns at bad grades, but for these children, her hug is even stronger. An invitation to come to her house for help with homework sounds more like an order. An eight-year-old smiles and shows Mary his loose front tooth. Now he has hope that his D in reading will improve. Besides, everyone knows that Mary always has food and candy, even clean clothes, mittens, and warm coats. But the children don't know that she lives hand-to-mouth just like they do.

Mary has had no income since she lost her job as a supervisor on a food canning line in 1991. For three months she was deeply depressed. Finally one morning she prayed, "God, you know I don't want to be like this. Show me what I should do." God was quick to guide her to the children, the most vulnerable people in her neighborhood; children of immigrants who don't speak English, children of families mired in the drug culture, and children of parents barely out of childhood themselves. Mary gained energy, renewed purpose, and, most of all, joy. When she had been employed, she used her free time to beg for food and clothing from local merchants for needy neighbors. Suddenly, her part-time charity became a full-time job. Now she runs a constant campaign for these necessities—and more.

"Kids need Christmas dinners, trips to the zoo, balloons, ice cream cones, and shiny new shoes," Mary says. She tunes out that little voice that nags, I deserve a new dress, a cozy bed, and reliable appliances, and points proudly to the donated provisions crowding her house: cans of food, disposable diapers, used clothing, and party supplies. Mary believes that all children should have a birthday celebration to remind them how special they are.

More than birthday cakes, she gives children who are forced to grow up too soon large doses of child-hood and the sense of self-worth that comes from knowing someone cares. Seventy-five percent of the kids in her neighborhood are high school dropouts, but not Mary's Kids. The coordinator of city youth services for the area has watched Mary in action for seven years. "Gangs? Drugs?" He shakes his head. "Not Mary's Kids. She won't hear of it."

How many kids does Mary have? Two of her own, both in their twenties. Her son is studying elec-tronics, and her

daughter is working on a
business degree. Of the
others, she loses
count, keeps no lists,
but thinks that on
average she cares for

about 150 youngsters at any one time. "What's going
to happen to the kids in the neighborhood if she's not
there when they need her?" her son asks. "That's all
that matters to her." His friends are surprised to see
where he lives, but he does not apologize. "It's what
my mom wants to do," he explains.

Mary's daughter would definitely like to live better. Her bedroom, like her brother's, is nearly empty,
yet their home is crammed with donated goods. "But,"
she says, "I want to do something like my mother is
doing with these kids."

Mary was raised not far from where she lives now.
She grew up on public aid, without a television or
telephone. Despite their family's poverty, her mother
always managed to share their food with hungry
neighbors. Mary learned charity at an early age, and
the lesson was reinforced every time her mother sacri-

ficed what little she had for a greater need. As an adult, Mary had struggles of her own trying to make ends meet, but when she saw a family living in a car, she knew she had to find a way to share. "My family had an income, a house," she says. Shamelessly and relentlessly, she began to lean on local merchants and neighbors to give what they could.

Now Mary has an abundance of time to give, time even for children whose names she does not yet know. They all seem to know her and are not surprised when she takes their hands and invites them to join the group of children around her. "Come on," she says. "It's too hot. We're off to buy ice cream." At 5'1" she is shorter than some of the children she befriends, but all of them look up to her.

For years, Mary worked out of her home. Her top floor was for the children. Craft projects, homework nooks, frequent parties, and games for kids of all ages kept many children off the streets and out of gangs that recruited members as young as nine years old.

Now, thanks to a $50,000 grant, Mary uses a field house in a local park for activities and has more resources to offer the children.

"She taught me to draw a flower," says one of Mary's Kids. "We made Mother's Day baskets and filled them with soap and perfume," shares another. A piñata is a little Hispanic boy's special memory. A young teen remembers going to a bowling party in a bus while a neighborhood gang set off on a vendetta against a rival gang. Another teenager recalls an all-day trip to the state capital. A favorite memory for many children is the time they had a shaving cream battle—Mary's creative solution when game and craft supplies ran low. The person who donated the shaving cream probably envisioned a more traditional use for it, but Mary sets the priorities.

Mary does not like the paperwork and preplanning required by the grant. She prefers the spontaneous ideas that grow from the moment. But despite the organizational requirements,

Mary puts her own spin on unexpected challenges and opportunities.

During a party at the park, a few of Mary's Kids began throwing stones at a homeless man trying to take a nap under a tree. Mary did not preach or threaten the children with no more parties. She simply invited the man to eat with them and seated him between two rock throwers. What the children remember most about the party is not the games they played or even the name of the ragged man who shared their birthday cake. The lesson that a lifetime of living will not erase is the memory of Mary taking off her socks and helping the homeless man pull them onto his cold and blistered feet.

*I will send an angel before you.*

Exodus 33:2

# Angel by My Side

As THE EIGHT-PASSENGER van rushed along the interstate, the darkness of the night matched the despair cloaking my heart. In the car lights flashing past, I glanced at the faces of the people surrounding me in the crowded van. Three men and two women, all of whom had difficulty with the concept of adding two plus two, but I could see in their eyes  that they understood the meaning of death. Don rocked rhythmically, twisting his hands over and over; George and Margo stared silently into the night; Sally's head was resting on Carl's shoulder for comfort, but her eyes were wide and fearful.

I couldn't bring myself to look at the far rear corner of the van—Robert's usual seat. What had started out as a fun-filled, week-long holiday for a group of mentally challenged people had turned terribly tragic when Robert, a 41-year-old man with Down's syndrome, died unexpectedly of a massive heart attack.

It was just after evening prayer. I'd been director of a group home for mentally challenged adults for ten years. The mission of our small community is to provide homes where adults with mental disabilities can live with dignity, respect, and, most of all, love.

The core members live as a family—cooking, cleaning, eating, and praying together. Robert had been with us since he was 18, the very first core member when our community opened its doors in 1974. Others soon followed, and the community grew to 18 men and women with nine live-in assistants—all of whom I was responsible for.

Was it only last week that we left for Kansas City? I could remember the excitement—the talking and laughter—as the group climbed one by one into the van for the trip.

"Colleen, are we going to the baseball game?" Sally asked, her toothless mouth shaped into a perpetual smile.

"Yes," I told her for the tenth time. "We're going to see a baseball game." I knew it was her favorite thing. She beamed.

"I want to go swimming," Don announced. The others were just as happy, giggling and laughing aloud. I was glad to see them do something that any person would do. It was my goal, the goal of our community, to make their lives as normal and happy as possible.

We'd been in Kansas City just a day. All of us—Carol, the assistant traveling with us, the six core members, and I—had spent the entire time at a huge amusement park where we enjoyed every minute. We rode the roller coasters, slid down tall slides on a plastic mat, played games of darts, and threw baseballs. I'd rarely seen the core members so happy. Carol and I laughed with them.

After we went back to the motel, we ate a decent supper at a very nice restaurant within walking distance of where we were staying. As was our evening practice, we held hands in the motel room and said our evening prayers. When we were saying our goodnights, and some of us stood to go to our respective rooms, Robert hesitated, put his hands on his chest, and then dropped to the ground. His eyes expressed total bewilderment. We immediately knew it was serious. I dropped to my knees next to him while Carol ran to call for help.

Margo was crying softly. "Robert ain't gonna die, is he?" she sobbed. "He can't die."

The others were frozen with fear and confusion. I watched the life drain from Robert's eyes as the sirens screamed toward us. I held his hand until the paramedics pushed me away.

The rest of the night was a blur. I began sinking into a despair such as I'd never felt before. Even though I knew in my heart

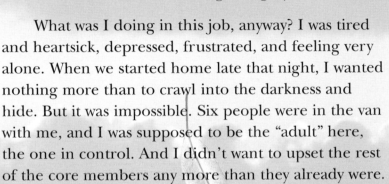

there was nothing I could have done to stop the dying, I felt guilty because I couldn't. I was angry with God because he allowed this to happen. Robert had been such a quiet, gentle soul. We called him "a man of the heart." *He deserved more,* I thought angrily.

What was I doing in this job, anyway? I was tired and heartsick, depressed, frustrated, and feeling very alone. When we started home late that night, I wanted nothing more than to crawl into the darkness and hide. But it was impossible. Six people were in the van with me, and I was supposed to be the "adult" here, the one in control. And I didn't want to upset the rest of the core members any more than they already were.

Thank God Carol had agreed to drive. My hands were trembling so hard that I knew I couldn't hold on to the steering wheel. I put my head down on the back of the seat in front of me and started to cry, pleading with God. "What am I going to do?" I asked silently. "Please help me."

At that moment an arm reached around my shoulders, a hand gently took my hand and a head rested against mine.

"Colleen, I'm going to pray for you." The words were whispered into my ear. At that moment I felt the presence of God. It was as if Jesus was sitting there with his arm around me. In my weakest moment, God came to me in the person of Don, one of our core members. The pain that I was feeling did not leave me, but now I knew I was not alone. I knew that God was with me.

A warmth spread throughout me, pushing the cold anguish to a corner of my heart.

"Thank you," I breathed. And in the darkness, I felt Don's smile.

*An angel on my shoulder*
*whispering in my ear,*
*telling me not to worry*
*for he is always near.*

# A Life-Changing Delivery

WHEN YOU THINK no one believes in you, it's hard to believe in yourself. Kevin Anson, a handsome young minister and single dad raising three children in Michigan, would be the first to agree with this statement.

Kevin's childhood was spent in a household dominated by a distant and disapproving stepfather. His stepdad was a college professor who never said a kind word to the boy. Although he was careful not to criticize Kevin too severely in front of his mother, whenever she wasn't around, the stepfather told Kevin he would never amount to anything. "You're too stupid to go to college," he would sneer. "Don't even try."

Kevin quickly lost interest in studying. As

high school graduation approached, his mother urged him to enroll in the local community college, but Kevin kept putting it off. Meanwhile, his stepfather was pressuring him to leave. "It's high time you supported yourself," he snapped. Kevin agreed. He could not endure his stepfather's ill-concealed hostility much longer, so he found a job as a cashier in a supermarket and moved out on his own.

Life in the outside world is anything but friendly to a teenager with no job skills, little education, and no experience fending for himself. It's hardly surprising that Kevin felt lonely and insecure on his own. Soon he began looking for companionship.

Jenny was a dark-haired, blue-eyed beauty three years younger than Kevin. A junior-high dropout from a broken family, she'd been moving from one boyfriend's house to another to keep a roof over her head. Jenny was a great deal more street-savvy than Kevin, and she used her flirtatious charms to get whatever she needed—food, clothing, or a place to stay. She was a troubled

soul, but Kevin didn't see that. He saw a
bubbly, fun-loving girl who seemed to
be fascinated with him.

Soon Jenny moved into Kevin's
apartment. She introduced him to
a host of friends, all streetwise
young people like herself, who
never held jobs for very long but
somehow managed to keep a sup-
ply of drugs and alcohol on hand.
When they partied late into the
night and Kevin found it difficult to get up for work,
Jenny would urge him to stay home. "If they fire you,
you can always get another job," she would coax.
Kevin began to lose job after job, to find that he
couldn't pay the bills, and to move from place to place
when the overdue rent eventually mounted up.

When Jenny discovered she was pregnant, Kevin
promptly married her. He felt they should begin living
a calmer life, one that would be healthier for raising
children, but Jenny didn't want to settle down. Within
four years they had three children, but motherhood
never slowed down the party-loving Jenny. Her erratic
behavior—leaving Kevin and the kids from time to

time so she could live with some new boyfriend or other—interfered with Kevin's attempts to create stability for his family. When their third child was only a few months old, Jenny left Kevin and the children once again. This time Kevin didn't want her back.

Barely into his twenties, with three tiny, dependent children to care for, Kevin realized he had to become a responsible adult. He would need to find a decent full-time job—and be sure to keep it. After some searching, he landed a job at a plant that produced foam cups. He'd had some experience in previous jobs as a machinist, so the plant hired him for a skilled trades position.

Kevin's supervisor was Dick West, a gruff but fatherly man who never missed an opportunity to let his workers know when they were doing a good job. As the months went by, Dick had many positive things to

say about Kevin's work. This was a priceless blessing, because Kevin desperately needed to hear that he was doing all right.

Kevin wasn't used to holding a job for more than a few weeks at a time. The daily grind made him impatient. He had to rise early and take his children to the babysitter before heading to the plant to put in a long day. Then he came home to make supper, do laundry, bathe the children, and read bedtime stories. He fantasized a thousand times about quitting his job and sleeping in as late as the kids would let him.

But he couldn't disappoint Dick. Dick said Kevin was a fast learner, a careful and precise worker, the best machinist they'd had in a long time. And Dick cared about how things were going with Kevin. He asked Kevin about his three children. He chuckled at stories about mischievous things they'd done and comical things they'd said. He commiserated with

Kevin about the everyday trials of broken water heaters and cars that refused to start. "It won't always be like this," Dick insisted. "Things will get better. I was a single dad myself in a situation like yours. But I survived—and you will, too."

Two days before Christmas, Kevin was at work, busily honing a tool, when Dick walked up to him. "I have a delivery to make outside the plant. Why don't you come along?" Kevin was puzzled; he'd never been asked to do this kind of work before. But if Dick needed help, he was happy to pitch in. Soon they were leaving the plant in a pickup truck. Kevin couldn't see what the truck held; its cargo was covered by a large tarpaulin.

Every time Kevin asked a question about their destination, Dick changed the subject. Kevin grew suspicious; the scenery looked familiar. In fact, they were practically at the trailer park where Kevin lived. As the truck turned into the park's entrance, Kevin said, "We're going to my place, aren't we?" Dick only grinned as he pulled up in front of Kevin's trailer.

When the tarpaulin came off of the truck, Kevin stared in amazement. The truck bed was loaded with brightly wrapped Christmas presents, tricycles for the kids, and enough fixings to make several holiday dinners. There was even a real Christmas tree and a box of decorations.

Every year at Christmas, the factory chose several families of employees who could use an extra boost. Dick had submitted Kevin's name and then discreetly collected all the information Santa's elves needed, such as the children's ages, genders, interests, and clothing sizes.

The Christmas truck was a turning point in Kevin's life because it brought more than gifts. It proved to him that someone recognized his potential and his hard work—that someone believed in him. Eventually Kevin became the chief machinist in his division, and he now owns his own home. His life has become more secure in other ways, too. Soon after that Christmas, he began attending church and received a calling to study for the ministry. Kevin has just been ordained as the pastor of his own church, where his mission is to offer others the belief that turned his own life around.

*I call upon God for comfort and solace,*
*He sends me angels to answer my plea.*
*They gently mend my broken heart,*
*And I am at peace in the world and one with heaven.*

*Let an angel into your life,*
*and joy and laughter will*
*follow you wherever you go.*

# My Son's Angel

WAITING IN THE school's parking lot with the windows down and the radio playing softly, I was enjoying the warm summer night. My son's face was beaming as he walked toward my car. I had to smile, too. I could see that Adam was brimming with news about the eighth-grade graduation dance he'd just attended. Adam always rushed home from school, erupting with stories before the screen door had even slammed behind him.

"I did the coolest thing I ever did in my whole life," he exclaimed as soon as he put one foot in the car. Very strong words from a person who's been in existence for just under 14 years.

The story just spilled out of him. "I was standing with Justin and Mark and Kristen and Britney," he began. "The music was loud and the gym was dark, and most kids were dancing and

laughing. Then Britney pointed out a girl who was standing off in a corner, crying.

"So Britney goes, 'You should dance with her, Adam.'

"I told her no because first of all, I didn't even know the girl. I didn't know her name or anything. But then Britney started bugging me even more. She told me I had a responsibility to people because of being class president. She said I should be a role model and that I had a chance to do something really special if I danced with this girl."

"Did you dance with her?" I asked him.

Adam was not going to leave out a single detail. "No, Mom. Not then. I told Britney that we didn't even know for sure why the girl was crying. That's when Britney said, 'Adam! Look at her. It's her eighth-grade graduation dance, and she's standing alone in a corner. No one is going to ask her to dance, and she knows it. Maybe she isn't thin or beautiful, but she's standing in a room full of her classmates, and they're ignoring her. They care only about what they're wearing and how they look and who they're with. Just think about how long you spent trying to decide what you were going to wear here tonight. Well, she did the same thing. Only no one is noticing and no one cares. Here's your chance to prove you deserved to be voted class president.'"

"So did you?" I asked. He looked at me with a not-so-fast-Mom frown, and I settled back into my seat to listen to more of the story.

"No," he said. "I knew Brit was right, but I kept thinking all my friends would laugh at me if I danced with her. So I told Britney, 'No way, I'm not doing it.'"

"What did she say to that?" I asked.

"Well, you know Britney. She wouldn't stop nagging me. She told me that if my friends laughed at me because I danced with her, then they weren't really my friends in the first place.

"I knew she was right. But it was still hard to go over and ask the girl to dance. What if I walked all the way across the gym in front of everyone and she turned me down? I'd die right there. But Britney said,

'She won't turn you down, and even if she does, you'll get over it by tomorrow. But I promise you, if you dance with her, she'll remember this night 20 years from now. And she'll remember you for the rest of her life.'

"So I went over to the girl and asked her what her name was. It was Janie. I didn't mention that I saw her crying, but I asked her if she wanted to dance. She said yes and as we walked out to the dance floor, I know my face turned red, but it was dark and I don't think anyone noticed. I had been so sure everyone would be looking at me, but no one laughed or anything and we danced the whole dance.

"Britney was right. It was three little minutes, but it made me feel really good. After that, a lot of the guys danced with her and with other girls who hadn't danced yet. It was like the coolest eighth-grade graduation dance. Everyone had a blast.

"I really learned something tonight, Mom."

*So did I, Adam,* I thought. I learned that a 14-year-old girl can be filled with compassion. I learned that peer pressure can sometimes be a good thing. I also learned that my son doesn't need me to teach him all of life's lessons anymore.

Yes, that night my son did the nicest thing he'd ever done in his 14-year life, and I'm proud of him for it. The remarkable child, however, was Britney. With one push of encouragement she changed, if only momentarily, the lives of a lot of kids. She helped give one sad girl a happy memory. She helped my son grow up a little. She challenged a bunch of teenage boys to reconsider what's really "cool." And she changed me, too. I always saw her as just another one of Adam's friends. Now I see her as his angel.

*Wrap yourself in the wings of an angel, and you will find peace.*

# Angelic Rescuers

*Now I am sure that*

*the Lord has sent his*

angel and rescued me.

Acts 12:11

# A Memorable Day at the Lake

HAT LONG-AGO day I remember looking up, seeing the sunlight dancing high above me through the greenish water mixed with silt from the lake's bottom. *I'll never make it,* I thought. As the rays of sunlight filtered through, I saw diamond sparkles swirling in the deep, and I recall thinking, *So this is what it's like to die.*

That summer morning at Meadowbrook Lake was typically hot and sticky. Though I was only 11 years old, this day would be burned into my memory forever—the day I knew without a doubt that angels were watching over me.

I spent the early morning at the edge of the lake with an oversize

glass trying to swoop up a
fish. First, I placed a ball
of bread inside the glass
and, while sitting in a
foot of water, I eased the

glass down. Then I waited until a curious fish swam in.
Just as it did, I jerked my glass out of the water and—if
I was quick enough—I'd catch a fish.

I had played this game several times with Billy, a
bully who lived near the lake, and I ended up beating
him every time. I saw the anger growing in his eyes,
and I knew he was embarrassed that a girl had beat
him. His neck and face grew tomato red with frustration. Although it was obvious he was mad, I never
dreamed how he would get even.

In the era of *Father Knows Best* when most mothers
stayed home, my mother worked. Since my eight-year-
old sister and I were often left alone, she occasionally
drove us to the lake on summer mornings and picked
us up after work. So that summer day my sister and I
were on our own except for a few sunbathing families.

Tired of catching fish, I decided to sit on the
sandy beach and build a sand castle. With the utmost

care I built a moat around my castle and dribbled wet sand over the top of the steeples. My sister offered to make it pretty by sprinkling each steeple with dry white sand. About an hour later, we stood back and admired our handiwork.

In less than a heartbeat, I saw someone racing toward my newly made sand castle. Billy screamed "Geronimo!" just before he jumped into the middle of it, scattering sand like fragments of sun-flecked glass. I was so angry that I chased him across the beach and up the hill to the clubhouse. Then I lost sight of him. As the day wore on, I figured he'd gone home.

Feeling the burning sun on our backs, my sister and I found shelter beneath a sweet gum tree where we ate our sandwiches and potato chips. As we downed our sodas, we talked about the sand castle, its early demise, and how angry we were with Billy.

Easing back into the cool lake water, I showed my sister a perfect round of ten forward underwater flips.

Squeezing water from my ponytail, I looked at my younger sister and said, "I bet I can swim out to the raft and back five times without stopping."

She grinned at me and said, "I bet you can't."

I was determined to show her I could do it. It was 500 yards out to the raft where the murky water stood more than 15 feet deep. I knew I could do it because I had mastered all the swimming strokes and even won a small trophy for the Australian crawl the year before.

I took a deep breath and dove into the water. When I broke the surface, I eased into the Australian crawl, taking one easy stroke, then another, until I was effortlessly gliding through the water.

I swam the crawl all the way out, touched the raft with my right hand, mentally said *One,* and then swam back to shore. Before my feet even touched bottom, I turned and started swimming back out. My arms felt heavy, so I turned over and began to float, letting my kicking legs carry me to the raft's side.

"Two," I said triumphantly, as I touched the side of the raft. Since no one was on the raft, I kicked off powerfully from its side causing it to sway. My breathing became ragged, and I slowed it by swimming on my side. When I reached the shore again, I glanced around the beach, but I didn't see my sister. I stood there for a few seconds catching my breath.

*Well,* I thought, *three times out there and back is not too shabby.* I shielded my eyes against the glaring sun and looked at the faraway raft, which was still empty. After a long, deep breath, I began the crawl once more to the raft.

As I neared the raft, I heard someone splashing near me. Before I knew it, Billy's face was inches from mine as he grabbed the top of my head with both hands. He shoved me under. Already winded, I fought to reach air. As I broke the water's surface, I gasped, and air as cool as a mountain stream

rushed in. Then Billy pushed me under again.

This time it was harder to reach the surface. My arms and legs felt like heavy weights. I struggled, kicking as hard as I could to once more fill my lungs with the sweet taste of air. As I reached the surface I tried to swim to the raft, but Billy was back in my face again.

He gritted his teeth, his eyes flashing anger. I flailed my arms at him trying to get away. But with both hands on my head, he thrust me under the water again. Then he did the unthinkable—he pushed me farther under with his feet until he was almost standing on my shoulders.

With my lungs about to burst, I instinctively began kicking, trying to reach the surface, but the struggle had exhausted me. This time, I didn't know if I could make it back up. Time slowed to a crawl. Everything seemed to be in a slow-motion dance— including me.

I remember looking up, seeing the sunlight quivering high above me through the hazy water. *I'll never make it,* I thought. Rays of sunlight bounced on specks of silt, then filtered through the green, reaching down to me. As I continued my battle upward, I noticed diamondlike sparkles all around me. They seemed to caress me. It was indescribably peaceful. I recall thinking, *So this is what it's like to die.* It was so beautiful and comforting beneath the water that I was almost content to stay there. But God had other plans for me.

I broke through the water gasping wildly. I could not seem to get enough air into my aching lungs. Then I heard someone calling from the raft, "Give me your hand!" I stretched toward the voice. The man caught my hand and dragged me toward the raft just seconds before Billy reached me again. With one last angry splash at me, Billy turned and swam back to shore. On the raft, I sat for what seemed an eternity, spitting up water and gasping. *Where did this man come from?* I wondered.

I know, for a fact, there was no one on the raft as I swam out, yet when my life was in mortal danger, a man seemed to appear from nowhere.

I'll never really know how the man got there, but I do know God commands angels to guard his children. A lifetime later, I don't know whether the man was sent from heaven or not, but it doesn't matter. He was an angel who was watching over me.

*Angels have appeared at every stage in the evolution of humankind. They've led the way of kings, and they've witnessed miracles. They've protected humanity and run errands for God.*

# The Mysterious Firefighter

WOMEN IN THEIR forties just don't get record deals. That's what Felicia Cole's best friend, Marly, had told her.

As Felicia stood at her mailbox that morning holding another rejection note and returned demo tape, she sighed with resignation. Maybe Marly was right. Maybe becoming a singer/songwriter was just a pipe dream, a possibility for someone far younger and more resilient than Felicia.

Felicia went into the small duplex she owned and closed the door behind her. She stared at the tape, tempted to toss it into the trash, along with her dreams. Instead, she put it into the drawer of her hall desk and decided to take a long, brisk walk to burn off her frustration. She put on her sweats, grabbed her keys, and headed outside.

It was a beautiful day, and, before she knew it, Felicia had logged three miles. She slowed down once to let two fire engines pass, curious as to where they were heading. As she rounded the bend heading back home, she could see smoke rising into the sky. Whatever was burning was close.

Back on her street, Felicia's heart stopped cold. The smoke was pouring out of her neighbor's home, which was attached to hers. She ran full tilt through the fire trucks and the firefighters milling around. Ignoring their warnings, she flew past them to her front door, unlocking it and racing inside. One firefighter chased after her, urging her to get out, and Felicia could see why. The flames had already passed through the common wall and now her home was on fire.

She screamed above the noise of falling beams and hissing smoke that she had to find her cat, Macy. The firefighter followed Felicia into a back room, yelling for her to come with him, but Felicia was on the floor reaching under the bed, where Macy was hiding. As Felicia reached to grab Macy, she heard a groaning noise. Just two feet behind her the ceiling fell in, showering pieces of rubble and wood that now stood between her and the firefighter who scrambled to get her free.

As the flames made their way into the hall just outside the back bedroom, Felicia understood the stupidity of her move. She was trapped. But at least Macy had jumped out of her arms and had run to safety out the open window in the adjacent bathroom. The firefighter, who told her his name was Bill, shouted at her to stay still, that he was coming to get her. He asked her name, and talked to her in a comforting tone, telling her it would be all right.

But Felicia wasn't so sure it would be all right. Smoke filled the room and her lungs, and she fought to stay low to the ground. She began coughing violently, feeling weaker with each passing breath. Bill's voice seemed to be getting farther and farther away. But she could feel him gently pick her up and carry her in strong, capable arms through the fire and smoke. Then everything turned to blackness.

When she next opened her eyes, Felicia was in an ambulance on the way to the hospital. She kept asking about the firefighter who rescued her, but the paramedic kept working and looking at her quizzically. He assured her that all the firefighters were fine.

She spent the next two days in the hospital. When she was released to her mother's care, the first thing Felicia did, even before calling the insurance company, was to pick up a notepad and pen and write the first words of what would become a song called "Cover Me."

Cover me, in times of trouble,
Cover me, in times of despair.
In your heart I can always find comfort.
In your arms I have nothing to fear.

One month later, Felicia stood at the mailbox of the apartment she was renting until her home was rebuilt. This time, the letter was not a rejection; it was an invitation to go to Los Angeles to talk with a major record company about a possible recording deal. They had loved her song "Cover Me" and thought it had hit potential. Felicia rushed inside to call the name and number on the letter to confirm, but she then decided to do something else first.

At the local fire station, just three blocks away, she rang the bell. A young man answered. Felicia asked if she could speak to Bill. The young man gave her a funny look, answering that there was no Bill there. Felicia insisted, telling him she was the one Bill rescued from the burning duplex. The young man just shook his head, then motioned for her to come inside.

Felicia waited in the TV room. An older man walked in and introduced himself. He told Felicia that he had been one of the firefighters on duty the day of the fire, and he reiterated that there was no firefighter named Bill, or William for that matter, on the roster. He looked surprised when Felicia asked who, then, had carried her out of the building. He told Felicia that no one had carried her out, that she had crawled through the rubble and fire on her own, and that he and everyone present had thought it miraculous that she had made it out alive.

But there had been no firefighter named Bill.

Felicia was confused, but she thanked the man and turned to walk back home. *They had to be wrong,* she thought, *for she had seen his caring eyes and heard his comforting voice. She had felt the strength of his arms as he carried her over pieces of burning wood and through the suffocating black smoke.*

For the rest of that day Felicia wondered what indeed had happened to her. But in her heart she believed that an angel named Bill had saved her life.

Her angel had truly covered her in times of trouble.

# Angels to the Rescue

OUR DAUGHTER ROBIN'S pregnancy had been difficult from the start. We were getting increasingly worried because she and her husband lived two hours from the nearest hospital. In the final months, her doctor advised the young mother-to-be to stay with us in town near the hospital. Robin readily agreed. Complications could develop. The baby could come quickly. We all knew the risks, but we tried to focus on the result for which we had prayed: the arrival of Robin's first baby, our second grand-child.

My wife, Shirley, and I urged Robin to rest and take care of herself as we went about operating our small neighborhood convenience store. The morning the baby was born started like many others. I was up before 6:00 A.M. to open the store. Shirley was still sleeping, until she heard Robin's anx-

ious call. "Mom, Mom," Robin whispered. "I'm sorry to wake you, but I think maybe my water broke."

The baby is coming, Shirley realized, instantly awakened while remembering the doctor's warnings that everything could happen very quickly. Not reaching the hospital in time could endanger both Robin and the baby. "Don't worry," Shirley urged, fighting to sound calm even though her heart was pounding. "Just get ready and we'll go. I'll tell Dad."

I closed up the store and started the car. Shirley dressed hurriedly and went to check on Robin. She was in the tub. Not wanting to alarm her, Shirley had not passed along all the doctor's warnings. Now, as she tried to hurry the ungainly mother-to-be, she wished she had.

Precious minutes ticked away as Robin looked for the nightgown she had planned to bring and chose an outfit for the baby to wear home. Labor pains hadn't really started except for some twinges, but Shirley knew that didn't matter. Finally, Shirley couldn't stand it any more. "We have to go right now!" she said.

By then, Robin had begun to feel some stronger contractions. As we drove the nearly empty streets toward the hospital, the pains began coming one after another. Robin cried out in anguish, and I tried to concentrate on the road. As she attempted to soothe and reassure Robin, Shirley prayed. "God be with us! God be with us!" Shirley, who had always relied on her strong faith, repeated the prayer over and over.

Finally, I turned into the hospital drive and headed toward a lighted sign that said "Emergency." I had hoped to see white-coated attendants running out to meet us as they did on television, but the area looked deserted. I stopped the car and dashed for the door. It was locked! A sign said to use another entrance before 7:00 A.M. I checked my watch: 6:45. I had no idea where to go.

Shirley had opened the rear car door to help Robin out, but she couldn't get off the backseat. "It's too late, Mom," she sobbed. "The baby's coming."

Shirley kneeled next to the car and prepared herself

to deliver the baby. "God be with us! God be with us!" she prayed, hoping desperately that God would guide her shaking hands. She could see the top of the baby's head. Then, she saw the umbilical cord wrapped around its neck, tightening with each contraction.

*Oh, Lord! What do I do now?* Shirley thought, terrified. Just then, she felt a rush of air and heard something like the sound of wings. She raised her eyes to see an angel hovering above Robin. She blinked, but the beautiful, winged creature remained, smiling back at her.

To her own amazement, Shirley suddenly knew what to do. She calmly ordered Robin to stop pushing and deftly untangled the cord. In seconds, she was holding her wailing grandson. But Shirley knew the danger wasn't over. The complications the doctor had warned her about still threatened. We had to get help immediately.

Frantic, I pounded on the emergency room doors, but I didn't see anyone. I turned to run around the building and search for an open door. That's when I noticed the man in the white jacket.

"They're coming," the man said serenely. "Wait just a moment more, and they'll be here. Everything will be fine."

"Are you a doctor?" I started to ask. But just then, the doors burst open, and a pair of nurses rushed out. They ran for a gurney and wheeled Robin and the baby inside. *The man must have alerted the staff*, I thought, and I turned to thank him, but the fellow was gone.

Stunned and exhausted, Shirley and I waited silently to hear whether our daughter and grandson would be all right. In her mind, Shirley recalled the image of the angel. She knew without a doubt that everything would be fine. I wondered about that stranger and wished I could tell him how much his help had meant to us.

Robin's doctor had arrived by then. The smile on his face as he approached told us all we needed to know. "Are you folks trying to put me out of business?" the obstetrician teased.

"Not on your life. I never want to do anything like that again," Shirley declared.

Not until later did my wife and I discuss all that had happened. I listened, shocked, as Shirley described the angel. The stranger suddenly took on a new significance. "I wonder if..." I hesitated to finish the thought.

But Shirley knew instantly what had happened. Tears welled up in her eyes as she said, "God heard my prayer and sent his angels to help us."

Our grandson, Julian, a happy boy, turns 13 years old this summer. Shirley says, "Every time I see him, I thank God again. He's our little angel."

*What know we of the Blest above*
*But that they sing, and that they love.*

William Wordsworth

# Flat Tire

OT AND BITTER. Prickly and sweaty. Alienated and full of self-pity. That's how I felt. It was summer in the Deep South, and I was standing on the side of an isolated two-lane road in the middle of nowhere with the flattest-looking tire I'd ever seen. It certainly hadn't been a good day. It hadn't even been a good year.

Sitting down on the edge of the backseat, looking out at the pastoral nothingness, I felt exhausted. Only the sight of my three-year-old son, Ian, sleeping in the car seat beside me provided any relief from the feelings that were over-whelming me. God was handing me one stinking, rotten deal after another. I knew my faith was being tested, and I was flunking the test.

I had set out on the ill-fated 200-mile round-trip drive for a job interview with new tires on my freshly tuned-up car. *At least we would have a safe trip with no mishaps,* I thought. Wrong! The interview hadn't even gone well. So now I was on my way back home to a low-paying newspaper job, assuming I could ever get back on the road. I enjoyed my job, but I was tired of eating cereal three meals a day, of constantly worrying about money, and of feeling so unbearably alone all the time. Everything was a challenge, from finding decent child care to paying for medical insurance, from keeping my battered old car running to finding peace and contentment for even a minute. I was anxious, overextended, and desperate much of the time. It seemed that the harder I tried, the further behind I got. I wanted a break.

I knew our situation wasn't much different from that of a lot of single-parent families. But I criticized myself for not doing well and then criticized myself for feeling bad about my failures. It was a downward emotional spiral.

Even the bit of good luck I had recently took a sour turn. When I found out about the interview, it happened that a friend's family lived in the same town. They offered to take care of Ian while I went to the interview. But when I drove back to the pretty little farm to pick Ian up, he seemed happier than ever surrounded by a large and loving family—a family that I couldn't give him. I drove away feeling really depressed and angry. I couldn't even be glad that Ian had enjoyed such a nice day.

I took a swig of water from the thermos I had prudently brought along. Then, after checking on my son, I got the spare, an inferior-looking piece of rubber, out of the trunk, along with the tire iron and the jack. I got the car jacked up and then went to work on the lug nuts. My geriatric car had long since lost its hubcaps. I tried to turn the last rusty nut, but it would not budge. I was getting sweatier and more aggravated. My hand slipped, and I scraped the middle knuckle of my right hand. Blood gushed everywhere. I grabbed

some tissues and applied direct pressure, trying to remember when I'd had my last tetanus shot. I sat down next to Ian and gave in to my tears. Through my sobs, I asked God what I had done wrong. It wasn't just the tire, the heat, and the bad interview—it was my whole pathetic life and, even worse, the life I was giving my son.

Cars zipped by, and no one stopped. I just sat and cried. I was so overwhelmed, I didn't even hear two people approach. I was startled when I heard a woman's soft voice asking, "Are you all right?"

I was embarrassed to be caught crying. "My tire's flat, and I can't get the lug nut off."

"What did you do to your hand?" asked a male voice. I looked up into a face so scarred it was hard to look at him.

"The tire," I said, pointing to the culprit.

"You got water?" he asked.

I told him I did. He reached for the thermos and poured the cold water over my hand, then gently wiped it with the tissue. Reaching into his wallet, he pulled out an adhesive bandage and placed it on my knuckle. Not a word passed between us the whole time.

The young woman looked at Ian, who was sleeping soundly. "He's a cutie," she said, smiling. She was pretty, with an open, vivacious face. "Waldo will fix your tire. He's good at mechanical things."

Waldo was already loosening the lug nut. If I hadn't been so hot and tired, I would have felt a little humiliated, but I was too close to heat prostration to care. My son stirred. As soon as he opened his eyes and spotted the smiling woman, he started grinning.

"Your spare's real bad. You need to get a new one," Waldo said.

"Great," I muttered, "another problem."

The woman identified herself as Laurie. She played patty-cake and peekaboo with a delighted Ian while Waldo finished his labors.

"You're all set," Waldo said, a beautiful smile that brightened and softened his ravaged face.

"We've gotta go," Laurie said, waving good-bye to Ian. "It's almost time for supper and then we've got church."

"About a mile down the road," Waldo told me, "there's a service station. My friend Billy works there, and he'll fix you up with a good tire cheap. You gotta replace the tire I put on. It's really bad. Then you need to get a new spare, too. I'll call him from the house to let him know you're coming. You take care."

Waldo and Laurie ran off down the embankment toward a dilapidated mobile home park. Both of them turned and waved. I waved back.

When I got to the service station, Billy was waiting. He handed me a soda. "Waldo said to fix you up with a good used tire 'cause your spare's shot. I got one here I'll let you have for eight bucks. I won't charge you no labor on account of Waldo sending you." While he worked, he talked—Billy was a talker. He told me he had grown up with Waldo. They'd gone to Vietnam together. "He got hurt over there," Billy said. He took his greasy hands and made a circle motion over his face. "When he came back, he had to go through a lot of surgeries for his injuries. He was engaged to Laurie's sister, and she dumped him."

"And Laurie...?" I asked.

"Well," he smiled, "we all used to kid him before the war about Laurie having a crush on him. He always laughed if off 'cause he'd been going with her  sister since junior high. But when he came back, it was Laurie that was there for him. She'd visit him in the hospital. She'd read to him and sing songs for him. Then, when he got out, she'd drive him to his rehabilitation visits. Bit by bit, we all saw it coming—he just fell for that girl. They're planning to get married soon." He stood up. "You're good to go."

I thanked Billy. He said he always takes care of anyone Waldo sends his way. I wondered how many people Waldo and Laurie have rescued. A man who carries bandages, and a girl with a healing smile.

That was 20 years ago. And two decades later, I still remember those good Samaritans and their faces and voices as if it were yesterday. They fixed a lot more than a flat tire that day. They gave a brokenhearted young mother renewed faith in humanity and in herself.

*If honor be given to princes and governors . . .*
*there is far more reason for it being given to angels,*
*in whom the splendor of the Divine glory*
*is far more abundantly displayed.*

John Calvin, *Institutes of the Christian Religion*

# Stranger on the Train

I WAS BORN AT home in Wilmington, Delaware, on a Wednesday in 1917. The following Sunday, my 11-year-old aunt came over and took me to church, and I've been going to church ever since. I was my aunt's doll. Why my mother would trust an 11-year-old child to take care of me, however, I'll never understand.

When I was three years old, my parents decided to move to a farm in Maryland. They thought the move would be good for the children, but my aunt was heartbroken when I left.

My older sister and my baby sister flourished on the farm, but I didn't. For three miserable years, I had one cold after another, flu twice, pneumonia, and whooping cough. Finally, the doctor told Mama if they wanted me to live, they had better find some way to get me off of the farm. My mother asked my grandmother and aunt if they would take me. They were delighted.

In September 1922, I was five years old and ready to start school. Before I departed for Wilmington, I needed some new shoes. At the store, a man tried these beautiful high-topped laced shoes on me. They were the first new shoes I ever remember having. While in the store the clerk didn't make me walk in them so I assumed they were OK. He wrapped up the old ones, and I wore the new pair. I was so proud.

Mama and Daddy took me in the wagon to the train station. This was the first time I could remember riding a train. I was excited but also frightened. My parents couldn't go with me, so I had to go by myself. My mother kept telling me not to be afraid and that God would take care of me. My grandmother would meet me at the train station in Wilmington.

There were two big signs hanging around my neck, one on the back saying where I was from and one on the front saying where I was going. I looked like a package ready to be mailed. Everyone looked at me and smiled. My father didn't think much of the signs, but my mother felt they were important. It was a good thing she did.

Mama put me on the train and sat me next to a kind old gentleman who graciously helped my mother put the suitcase over-head. Then he offered me the seat by the window. Before Mama left, she told me again not to be afraid and assured me that God would take care of me. I was still very scared, but I tried to be brave.

After a while my feet began to hurt since I'd been walking in my new shoes. I started to cry. The man asked what was wrong. I told him my feet hurt, so he took off my shoes. My feet felt better right away.

In those days the train was a local. It stopped at every little station, and the trip took more than three hours. Men came around selling sandwiches and drinks, but my mother had packed a lunch for me. The nice man asked if I would like to have a soda.

I said, "No, I don't have any money." He bought me one anyway, and I drank it with lunch.

Soon the conductor started announcing that Wilmington would be the next stop. The man helped me get on my shoes.

When we arrived in Wilmington I waited for the Traveler's Aid to come and get me off the train. I waited and waited but no one came. Finally, the nice man said, "I'd better get you off. The train is about ready to leave." He grabbed my suitcase, picked me up, and carried me off the train just before it pulled away. I often wonder if he really wanted to get off at that stop.

The man sat on a bench with me and helped me look for my grandmother. No one was around. We continued to wait. The man had heard my mother talk about the Traveler's Aid when she put me on the train, so he took me to that office. The receptionist looked in her book but found no record that someone was supposed to meet me. She wanted to call my grandmother, but my grandmother didn't have a phone. (That was not so unusual in those days.)

The nice man decided to put me in a cab and send me to the address on my sign. He told the cab driver to see that I got there and to put me on the porch or set me on the steps. Then he told me not to move off the porch or steps if my grandmother wasn't home. He paid the cab driver and sent me on my way.

Fortunately my grandmother was home. When she saw me, she was shocked. She had not received the letter my mother had sent. It came later. It had gone to Wilmington, North Carolina, by mistake.

I have often thought about that nice man on the train. I think he must have been an angel God had sent to take care of me, just as my mother had promised. That lesson has always stuck with me. It makes me think of how God has taken care of me all these years.

*It's a comforting thought to know that*
*angels work and move among us*
*to make the most of the love we have.*

# Incident on the Bridge

WE ALL FACE a day of reckoning. We find ourselves there when we have run as far as we can, for as long as we can.

I had just finished writing my suicide note. I left it for my three daughters on the front seat of my car. I wanted them to understand, from my own words, what had driven me to this moment.

It was 1992. I'll always remember it as the worst year of my life. My one blessing had been a new baby girl, but even that happiness had come at great cost since we discovered during the pregnancy that something was seriously wrong with my heart. I had spent much of the pregnancy in the cardiac care unit of the local hospital. Right after my baby was born, I was moved to another hospital in another city for intensive care and diagnostics. Because my heart was extremely weak, the doctors would not let me hold my baby girl for a month and a half. It was a horribly lonely and difficult time for me.

Then, when I finally returned home, weak in body and spirit, I sensed that all was not well there, either. I learned that my husband had not brought our new baby home during my long stay in the hospital but had paid professional sitters to keep and care for her. And soon I heard rumors about my husband and another woman. But that couldn't be true, could it? The "other woman" was my best friend, someone I'd shared so much laughter, love, and sorrow with over the years. So I ignored the talk and tried not to notice the small signs that sometimes nagged at me. We maintained an uneasy peace for six months; my heart, after all, was still too weak for such a shock. But then one night, with our baby yet an infant and my health still fragile, my husband did not come home. My best friend, as it turned out, was with him.

I had been married to this man for 16 years! We had three lovely daughters, a comfortable home, and a business we had built ourselves, together. Suddenly,

I was alone, in my thirties, with a new baby and two teenage girls, a heart that was giving out, and a marriage that was over. All the security I'd known had been shattered.

I felt so alone, so rejected by the husband I still loved. Still loved! How could I? He'd abandoned me and, together with my best friend, had betrayed me. I begged God to take the love from my heart, but my prayers seemed to be in vain. I cried out to God, "Why have you turned your back on me?" I was physically and emotionally drained.

Was I searching for God's attention when I parked my car at 2:00 A.M. that Sunday morning? Maybe I was afraid he didn't love me, or maybe I was afraid he just might.

I knew there would be no traffic on the bridge leading out of town in the middle of night. No one would notice that I had slipped quietly away. I would jump into the river and let God do with me whatever he saw fit. As I climbed to the highest point on the bridge, I could feel the tears spilling down my cheeks and the breeze of the cool night air.

At the precise moment I stood up to leap, a hand touched mine and held it tight. I turned my head and saw a man, a stranger.

He said, "Lady, I don't know what's happening here, but as I drove over this bridge, something or someone said as plain as day: Turn around, now, and go back. I didn't want to go back, but all of a sudden my wheel started turning in my hand, and I couldn't make it stop. Then, as I was heading back over the bridge, I saw you. It must have been an angel who turned that wheel—it certainly wasn't me. So don't jump. Please don't jump. God sent me to hold your hand."

As he spoke, a sense of peace settled over me. I knew I was supposed to step back off that bridge.

I let the man help me down. When I looked up, police cars were all around us.

Over the next few weeks, as I began to recover, I felt ashamed that I had almost taken my life just because another human being had let me down. I now saw clearly that there was someone who had been there all along, someone who cared for me and promised to stay with me always.

But my difficulties were not over yet: I had a divorce to get through, I would have to stay on heart medication for the rest of my life, and I was a single mother with two teenagers and a baby. But in spite of all this, the peace I'd felt that night on the bridge— when a stranger stood next to me, holding my hand and talking about God's love—stayed with me. I felt a new sense of security, a different, deeper security that sprang from a renewed trust in God, from a certainty that, somehow, our lives would be all right.

After that, the pieces of my life started to fit into place. I began to gain insight into what had gone wrong. I was able to let go, to start over emotionally, to stop dwelling on the past. And, with the Lord's help, I was able to learn forgiveness. That was perhaps the hardest task of all, but I eventually truly forgave both my husband and my friend, and it's a wonderful feeling to have that resentment taken away. There is no end to what the Lord has done for me; every day I see him at work in the lives of my three wonderful daughters.

I've tried many times to find out something, anything, about the man who helped me that night on the bridge. I often think about him; I wish I could thank him for saving my life. But no one remembers him. The police don't recall talking with him, nor was he mentioned in any police reports. He never told me his name, and I can't remember much about what he looked like. I think he had brown hair and brown eyes, but I'm not even sure about that. He was just an average man, guided by God's angels to help an average woman. God reached out to touch two ordinary hearts on a bridge that night, and both of us learned of God's extraordinary love.

*Angels move in mysterious and wonderful ways.*
*They speak with hushed and holy voices, and in warm*
*and gentle tones. Their loving presence and kind words*
*cover us with peace and comfort.*

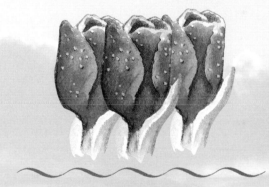

*If you listen carefully you may hear,*
*An angel whispering softly in your ear,*
*With a voice like the coo of a dove,*
*Whispering of God's perfect love.*

# Truck Lights in the Night

WHENEVER MY SAILOR husband was assigned to sea duty, I would stay with my mother in Brownwood, Texas. During one such visit in 1954, we drove to a family reunion with my two daughters, Faye, three years old, and Sissie, almost two. When the reunion ended, the weather looked stormy, but we decided to head home anyway.

The highway took us through small towns and rural areas of Texas. Momma wanted to stop at Wiley, the all-black college where I received my degree in biology in 1947. To pay for my schooling, Momma had worked as a pastry chef, and Wiley was a monument of sorts to the years she spent baking hundreds of pies, cakes, and cookies.

We had a ten-hour drive ahead of us, however, and dark clouds were gathering.

The temperature was falling, so we stopped to put sweaters on the girls, and Momma sat in the backseat between them. Opening the box of sandwiches we had brought along, she passed one to me and said, "Don't worry about us. We're as warm as toast."

Nevertheless, I was worried. It was hard for me to see. If I had known then that I had night blindness, I would have tried to find a place to stop. But being black meant that we could not just pull into a motel and wait out the storm. Segregation still prevailed.

When night came, the falling snow curtained off the sky. Not even the moon and stars were visible. When I pulled into a truck stop to get gas, I told the station attendant that I could scarcely see the road. He was very concerned when he realized I intended to keep driving that night.

Foolishly, I got back in the car with my mother and my two babies and started out again. I soon realized I could not see the road. It was as though we were in a dark cave, and I began to panic. I couldn't see to go forward; I couldn't see to turn around. Pulling off to the side of the road was out of the question, as I could not see that either. I wasn't even sure that I was on the road!

I tried to pray, but I was almost paralyzed with fear. Briefly, I put my head on the steering wheel and rubbed my eyes in hopes of seeing better. When I looked up, I saw lights approaching in the rearview mirror. The lights turned out to be from two 18-wheelers. One drove around in front of my car and slowed down. The other stayed behind us, its lights casting a welcome glow inside the car. I knew in my heart that the man at the gas station had told those truckers about my predicament, and they had decided to help. God had answered the prayer I could not utter.

I nestled between the hovering vehicles like a chick taking refuge under its mother's wings. We traveled for some time this way, and then I saw the right-turn signal light blinking on the leading truck. The driver flashed his headlights several times as a way of saying good-bye before he turned onto another road. For a moment I was terrified to be back in the darkness, but then the truck that had been behind me pulled out in front and continued to act as my guide.

It was dawn when we got back to Brownwood. I blew my horn and waved at the trucker. He lowered his window and smiled as he waved back. I never knew the names of those drivers who helped deliver us safely home, but I will be forever grateful for the help they gave us on that dark and stormy night.

*If you have the good fortune to be surprised by an angel, you will enjoy a delightful, lingering sense of the divine. Indeed, your life will never be ordinary again.*

# Angelic Voices

*angel*

The angel said to them,

"Do not be afraid;

*afraid*

for see —I am bringing

*news*

you good news of great

joy for all the people."

*joy* Luke 2:10

# The Voice

SOMEHOW MY GRANDPARENTS, who were raising me, and I managed to survive the ravages of World War II in our native Hungary. But when that terrible war finally ended in 1945, no jubilation arose because Soviet troops immediately held our country hostage in the arms of communism. Suddenly, people who had spoken out against the new oppressions taking place were soon rounded up by the recently formed secret police force, and they were never seen again.

My grandfather, a retired judge, continued to speak out, and, in the fall of 1945, two men appeared at our house to take him away. They said he was being taken in only for questioning. Grandfather, pointing out that his hands were dirty from working in the garden, asked if he could first wash up. The men agreed. When he didn't come out of the bathroom right away, the men ran and pushed the door open. The water in the sink was still running, but Grandfather was gone. He had jumped out the bathroom window and fled on foot.

After Grandfather went into hiding, life became even more difficult for Grandma and me. We lived on soup made from the potatoes and other vegetables grown in our garden, and we never knew when the secret police would show up again to search our house. Sometimes they came in the middle of the night, breaking down the door in hopes of finding Grandfather. Fear became our constant companion and prayer our sustenance.

For two years my grandfather managed to elude capture, and, although he sent word to us of his safety, most of the time we did not know his whereabouts. Grandma and I missed him terribly. The thought that we might never be together again plagued me constantly. But on an autumn day in 1947 when I was ten years old, it seemed as though the time had come for us to be reunited.

When new elections were held in our country, I waited for the results with great interest. The next morning our radio announced that the communist party had been defeated. Celebrations erupted in the streets, with none of us realizing that the communist government, backed by Soviet troops, wasn't about to give up that easily, elections or no elections.

Certainly, after listening to the radio broadcast, my ten-year-old mind concluded that the election results meant that Grandfather could come home and we could be a family again. I wondered if Grandfather, who we recently learned was hiding out on a nearby farm, had heard the good news. I decided now was the time to hike to the farm and tell him. Then we could

come home together and surprise Grandma! Of course, I didn't tell anyone of my plan. Rather than go to school, I set out on the long walk out of town to Grandfather's hiding place. As I reached the outskirts of our village without having drawn any attention to myself, wild antic-

ipation filled my
heart. In a short
while I would see
Grandfather for the
first time in two
years, and we would

walk home together and live as a family again. My eyes
filled with tears of joy, and I began to walk faster.

Suddenly I was startled when I heard a man's
voice call my name. I stopped dead in my tracks and
looked all around, but I saw no one. "Who are you?
Where are you?" I asked quietly, straining to see if he
might be hiding in some nearby bushes.

"It isn't important where I am," the voice replied.
"I am here to warn you that you are putting your
grandfather in grave danger, for you are being followed. Turn around and go back to your grandmother
immediately, and know that you will all be together
again soon."

Frightened now, I immediately turned and began
running back toward the village. My heart was pounding so hard I thought it would jump right out of my
chest. I ran past a man on a bicycle and recognized

him as one of the secret police. The stranger's voice had been right: I was being followed!

When I reached our house, I found Grandma outside pacing back and forth in the street. "Oh, thank God, you are all right!" she cried, gathering me in her trembling arms. "They came to tell me that you were not in school, and I thought someone had taken you away."

"I decided to go and tell Grandfather that the communists lost the election," I wailed. "I thought we could come home together and surprise you!"

"Oh, my!" Grandma said, shaking her head in disbelief.

"But someone stopped me," I continued. "A voice told me I was being followed and that I should go back home. It was the kindest, most loving voice I have ever heard, Grandma. I believe it was the voice of God speaking to me. No one else knew of my plan. No one!"

My grandmother nodded silently, ushered me into the house, and continued to hold me for a long time. Then she reassured me that everything would be better soon.

Two weeks later, a man came to get us in the middle of the night. By the time the sun rose, we had traveled many miles to a place near the Austrian border where a large group of ethnic Germans was about to be deported into Austria. My heart leapt when I saw Grandfather there. He looked lovingly into my eyes and hugged me tight. We were to be smuggled out of our country as ethnic Germans. Recognizing the danger still around us, we didn't dare breathe a sigh of relief until we crossed into Austria. There, we ended up in a refugee camp along with hundreds of other destitute refugees, but at least we were finally together again.

Grandfather remained fearful that the long arm of communism could still reach out and snatch him back. It wasn't until 1951 when we were given a chance at new lives in our wonderful new country, the United States of America, that he was finally able to relax and live out his life in peace.

Over the years, I have often wondered about the voice I heard on that fall day in 1947. I speculated that the voice might have belonged to some kind neighbor who had guessed my destination and decided to warn me anonymously. Or perhaps it really was the voice of an angel that prompted me to turn around. Whether the voice was human or heavenly, I know one thing for sure: God's hand guided us safely back together so we could be a family again.

*There are angels all around us,*
*Hidden, barely out of sight.*
*You may catch a glint of halo glow,*
*Or the rustle of a wing in flight.*
*There are angels all around us,*
*Though we rarely get to see,*
*That there are angels all around us,*
*Watching over you and me.*

# At God's Urging

CASSIE HAD BEEN a gospel singer, a songwriter, and had published a book, but when I heard about her, she was badly depressed. She had become disabled after being run down by a hit-and-run driver. Thus, she had gone from being fairly well-off to being a poor person who had to live in public housing and depend on other people to do her shopping and drive her where she needed to go. Not that she went out much—she was afraid she would get hit again. In fact, she was so afraid that she rarely left the house. Before she was injured, Cassie had attended church nearly every Sunday of her whole life, and she had sung in the choir since she was a child. But now she couldn't be coaxed from her home to attend the services she had loved so much.

Cassie had been a tall, heavyset woman to begin with, and after becoming disabled she spent a lot of time in her kitchen preparing large amounts of food and then eating all of it. As a result, she gained so much weight that she had nothing to wear. This only added to her depression. She wondered if God had abandoned her. Finally, she prayed that if God was still there and still loved her, he would show her a sign of his love and presence.

Cassie's niece is my friend and prayer partner. She told me of Cassie's plight and asked me to pray for her aunt. Since I am in charge of the clothing drive at my church, I told her that there probably would be some clothing in the upcoming drive that would fit her. A couple days later, my friend reported to me that she had told Cassie about it, and Cassie was excited about getting some "new" clothes. Just the idea of it lifted her spirits.

However, it turned out that there was nothing in Cassie's size in the clothing drive. I was disappointed, because I knew how important this had been to Cassie. I started to call my friend to tell her there was nothing available for her aunt, but then I got a

feeling that I was supposed to go buy a dress for Cassie. At the time, I did not know about her prayer.

I knew what God wanted me to do, but I resisted. Our finances were tight, and I didn't want to spend money on a dress for a total stranger. I fought the feeling for several days, but it did not go away. Finally, I knew that I needed to listen to God's urging.

I felt compelled to go to a certain department store, even though I don't usually shop there. When I arrived, I headed for the clearance section. I looked and looked, but there was only one dress in the right size that seemed appropriate for an older woman to wear to an air-conditioned church. The dress had been marked down 50 percent and was now $39.

I could do a lot with $39, so I was hesitant to spend that much money on this dress. I started to walk out of the store, but a voice inside me kept urging me to buy the dress.

I gave in and walked back to the rack. I picked up the dress, took it to the checkout line, and waited behind three other people. When it was my turn, I handed the dress to the cashier, and she scanned the price. The cash register started making one transaction after another. I'd never heard a cash register make such a racket or print out such a long ticket for one item. Even the cashier noticed it and said in a surprised voice, "I don't see how this one was missed being marked down that many times." The dress had been through many sales, but the ticket had been marked down only once. In the computer, however, it was marked down repeatedly until the final price was $2.97.

I couldn't believe it! I started saying, "It was the Lord! It was the Lord!" and I told everyone who was standing near me what had happened. They were all pleased to have witnessed the small miracle.

I had no intention of telling my friend or Cassie that I had bought the dress. I was just going to let them think that it had been in the clothing drive. But when I told my daughter about it, she said, "God blessed her by giving her a dress, and he blessed you by showing you a miracle. You need to tell them about it." So I did.

My friend tells me that the dress fits Cassie perfectly and looks very nice on her. She also credits the dress for getting Cassie on the road to recovery from her bout of depression. Just about everyone Cassie knows has heard about the miracle dress. On a Sunday not long after she got it, she sang a gospel solo at her church and told the whole congregation about her dress. They clapped their hands and praised the Lord.

This incident has strengthened my faith and has made me more generous and willing to do what God asks. That miracle dress has been a blessing, both for Cassie and for me.

*On gossamer wings they move as gentle breezes on a warm summer's eve, quietly reminding us that we are always being watched over, always being loved.*

# Alarm Bells

FALL HAD SETTLED over the community in a blaze of glory: maples, oaks with their purplish-brown leaves, the hawthorns with red berries clumped at the end of the branches.

It may have been the dry summer or the dusty, dry fall now under way that unleashed all the germs early, but it was the worst flu season in memory. Newscasters were predicting one of the worst winters for illnesses.

It had hit Sara the week before Halloween.

She had been sidelined for two days with a headache, cough, and fever. Finally, she had gone to the doctor, who, while he sympathized, was himself sneezing up a storm. He sent her home with pills and potions that "knocked her out," as she put it.

"At least while you're sleeping, you won't be coughing," said her husband sympathetically, pulling on his work gloves and hunting for the matches. "You rest," he advised. There was very little wind that day, and he was going out to rake and burn the leaves while she slept. "When I come in, I'll fix you a nice supper," he promised.

Sara smiled to herself as she lay down on the couch, pulling the quilt up to her chin. Her husband's idea of fixing a nice supper was opening a can of soup, heating the contents, and serving it on a tray with crackers arranged around the soup bowl like sunflower petals! But at least he was thoughtful and caring. That's what gave the soup he offered that special taste, that little extra something.

For 35 years he had been doing just such thoughtful things. She was a fortunate lady, if you believed half the tales you saw on TV or read in magazines. Or, she had to admit sadly, even if she listened to some of her friends.

Succumbing to the medicine's pull, she drifted off into a deep, drug-induced slumber with a smile on her face thinking of this special man puttering around the backyard with his rake and wagon. He loved being busy. Retirement had not slowed him down a bit; it just gave him more time to think up projects to accomplish.

Sara was sound asleep when someone started pounding on her back door. Groggily, she got to her feet. "I'm coming," she called, pulling on her bathrobe. In her confused haste, Sara tripped over the quilt. She gathered it in her arms to avoid falling.

"Hurry!" shouted the person at the door. When she opened it, however, there was no one there . . . only her husband out by the road burning leaves in the ditch. As she watched, he lost his balance and fell into the flames.

He couldn't get up.

It was as if Sara's bathrobe had wings. She got to the fire in time to pull him to safety and wrap him in the quilt she had been dragging.

"No," he told her later at the hospital, "I didn't see anybody in the yard or on the porch coming to get you. It was just my lucky day that you woke up when you did."

They held hands...until the nurse brought him his supper: soup that Sara fed him, after she blessed it with a prayer for its nourishment and with a thank-you to the angel who had given her more time with her husband here on earth.

*No matter the difficult people who cross our paths, there is goodness in this world. It is there because we are surrounded by the goodness of angels and the goodness they help us cultivate in ourselves.*

# Stranger in the Night

THROUGHOUT MY CHILDHOOD, I watched as my father and his brothers and sisters always welcomed an opportunity to help someone in need. One day I mentioned this to my grandfather, and he replied, "They were helped when they were very young, so the least they can do is share their blessings with others." My grandfather sat back in his recliner—a sure sign he was about to deliver a great story. . . .

"I was what you'd call an adventurous fellow in my day. Life was exciting, and opportunities seemed to abound for those who liked a challenge. But I married young and had to settle down, much to the sorrow of my pals. Joe, the real daredevil of the group, went out west to seek his fortune. In those days, Ohio was considered the west. His was a daring journey, with no turnpikes or any of the other roadside conveniences we have now.

"Several months after Joe headed west, I got a letter from him proclaiming his great regret that I had been foolish enough to get married so young and find myself tied down now with seven children. If not for my growing family, I could have joined him in Ohio, which he described as 'the land of milk and honey.'

"Apparently Joe had not counted on my reaction to his letter. I couldn't think of any reason why I couldn't pack up my family and go west, too. But when I arrived, the opportunities weren't as plentiful as Joe had said. And by then he had moved even farther west.

"With our funds dwindling, we couldn't follow Joe or even return home. We settled down in an old deserted house, which the local people thought was haunted. Day after day I looked for work of any kind, but times were bad and no one had any idea whether or not I would stick around.

"Your grandmother and I ate very sparingly, saving most of our food for the children. Even so, we reached the point of not having enough food even for them. Fortunately, the children always accepted any changes that came their way, so they readily agreed to my proposal that we do things a little differently one night. Since we were all tired and cold, I suggested that we circle around the stove in the kitchen, kneel down and say our evening prayers, then rush to bed. We would eat, I assured them, when we woke up.

"Shortly after midnight, we heard a pounding on the front door. When I opened the door, there stood a stranger with a huge basket of food. He seemed as surprised to see me as I was to see him, or perhaps it was the sight of so many wide-eyed children coming down the steps that gave him a shock. In any event, he said he was delighted to find people living in this house, because his wife would never let him hear the end of it if his trip had been in vain.

"He went on to say that each time he had fallen asleep that night, he'd heard a voice directing him to take food to the haunted house in the village. His wife told him it was only a dream and that if the neighbors saw him going out into the night with bags of groceries, they would think he was as crazy as a loon. Twice she persuaded him to go back to sleep, but when he heard the directive a third time, he got dressed and, despite his wife's jeer-

ing, loaded up all kinds of food and went out into the dark night."

Grandpa seemed rather shaken as he spoke of the experience. After a moment, he went on to say, "Now my children are grown and have children of their own. I hope they tell them about the stranger who came to our rescue that winter night. God works in mysterious ways. Perhaps someday they may be the instruments God uses to answer someone else's evening prayers."

*Throughout history angels have been our connection to heaven. There seems to be no protocol too fine or too unworthy for heaven's angels to touch down and offer their guiding light.*

# That Gentle Angelic Voice

THE WORDS OF the doctor echoed with unmerciful finality. He had been gentle and kind, and he had held me as I wept, standing patient and still as I beat my fists into his chest. But now he was gone, and I was left alone with my reality.

"Oh, God! Why? Why? Why would you allow this? Why him? Why me? Why now?" I shook my fist in the air and pounded on the windowsill. The pain and grief held my heart in a vicelike grip, so tight I gasped for air and felt as if my chest would explode. "You can't be doing this to me," my mind screamed over and over in silent anguish. "He is my son, my only child, and you can't take him from me. You can't!"

I made myself look one more time at the tiny figure in the crib. Tony was separated from me by two thick panes of glass. Such a beautiful son, so perfectly formed and so precious. "Oh, God!" I cried. "You have to let him live!"

Tony had been suffering from an extended high fever, and the doctors told me that even if he did live, which was doubtful, he would most likely be brain-dead. The thought of losing my son was too much for me to bear.

I walked out of the room into the quiet, sterile hallway. My shoes clicked on the shiny tiles as I made my way to the sliding door. Outside, rain hit my face and mingled with my tears. Gusts of wind pulled at me with determined force as I started to walk down the road. I had planned to go home, but somehow the thought of my empty house held me back.

I stumbled up the steps of an unfamiliar church. The heavy door made a sad scraping sound as I let myself into the dimly lit chapel. I made my way to the front pew and knelt down. Staring at the statues of Jesus and Mary, I suddenly felt an overwhelming desire to shout at God. I wanted to pray, but it seemed so helpless, so futile, so useless.

"You say to ask, and you promise you will hear," I whispered, "and yet my son is dying. Your Word says that you love us and see our tears. But do you really care? Do you care about a tiny, helpless baby or a brokenhearted mother? Are you too big, too far above us to hear our cries or see our pain? The Bible tells how you bid the little ones to come to you, and how you touched the sick, the lame, the blind, and the deaf. How, as you walked among men, they were healed with just a word or a glance. That same Bible says you are a God of love, a God who never sleeps, a God who shows mercy to all who call, a God who cares for and protects his little ones. Is that true?"

I sat there, staring through my tears at the statues before me. So intense were my grief and pain that I didn't hear a door open or see the elderly priest as he entered and quietly joined me

in the front pew. The hand, gently placed
on my shoulder, and his tender
words—"May I help you, child?"—
caused me to jump slightly as I
turned my startled eyes upon the
kind face of the priest.

I had come here to be alone with my anger and
to pour out that anger on a God who seemed far, far
away. I certainly didn't need anyone telling me fables
of God's love or offering to pray with me for the
Lord's mercy and grace.

I opened my mouth to say just that, but no words
came. Then suddenly, heavy sobs shook my body and
caused my breath to come in short, body-wrenching
gasps. I cried in anguish from my gut. For several
minutes, the priest sat beside me, gently holding my
hand. Then, as if a dam had broken within me, my
anger and pain poured out. I yelled shamelessly at the
priest, who made no effort to interrupt me or to stop
my avalanche of biting words.

The priest's eyes were filled with compassion, and
once I had stopped my tirade, he spoke to me in a
soothing voice. He talked of a gentle, loving, merciful

God who saw my grief and felt my pain. A Lord who understood the anger that poured from my lips and wanted to bestow merciful healing to my stricken, weeping heart. With his hand gently holding mine, this wise servant of God introduced me to a Jesus who is able to meet my every need. A Christ who loved me so much he was willing to allow the anguish I felt in order to bring about a complete melting within my spirit, a morphing of self-will into a more perfect Christ-will.

For a few moments all was quiet in the dimly lit chapel as I allowed the priest's words to echo through my mind.

Then softly, a gentle yet compelling voice seemed to speak to my spirit: "Let go! Please let go so I may bless you. Let me be Lord, and let me have control. I love you, I love your son, and I long to give you your heart's desire. But first you must let go." Suddenly I felt, for the first time ever, that I really was a child of the living, loving, all-knowing God. A God full of compassion and mercy. I thanked the priest, then left the church and headed home. The pain in my heart lessened with every step. "Oh, Holy Father," I whispered, "I surrender all to your loving hand. Tony is your child, and you love him far more than I ever could. I freely give him back to you."

Tony is now 34 years old. He graduated from high school with honors in 1984 and has become an accomplished chef. Every day of his life has been a blessing to me.

I'm so thankful to God for leading me to that gentle priest on a dark, rainy day when my heart and soul were aching. Thanks to the priest's kind, inspirational words, I was able to see that the deepest, purest love is the kind that can let go.

*When you feel lost, pause and look closely around you.*
*Somewhere, somehow, an angel will be waiting*
*to guide you home.*

# A Call from God

T WAS COMMON for me to go by the supermarket bakery on my way to work and have a fresh donut and a cup of coffee. Being single and usually in a hurry, eating out was the rule for me rather than the exception.

On this particular day as I walked into the bakery, I noticed a young woman (she looked to be in her early thirties) sitting alone at a table. She appeared to have just crawled out of bed after sleeping in her clothes all night. Tattered grocery bags were scattered around her feet. These bags were not filled with groceries from the market; rather they were filled with what appeared to be all her earthly possessions. I felt empathy for her but quickly brushed it out of my mind. I didn't have time to concern myself with a stranger.

After purchasing my donut and coffee, I glanced at the clock. I had 15 minutes to eat, drink, and drive the remaining five miles to work. I was right on time. From where I was seated, I could see the mystery woman. She had nothing to eat or drink on her table, and for a fleeting second, I thought it might be "a nice thing to do" to buy her some breakfast.

I immediately dismissed the thought. After all, this was the big city, and the sight of a street person was common. And I, a young executive-type, was in somewhat of a hurry. Besides, I told myself, people are just asking for trouble by approaching strangers. I forgot all about her.

Right on schedule, I finished my breakfast and got up to head for work. Passing the woman, I could not help but notice how forlorn she looked sitting there, staring off into space. Many thoughts raced through my mind: *I wonder if she's hungry. Probably mentally ill. Most of them are. Looks as though she's had that same dress on for a week. No telling how long it's been since she's had a bath. But she's one of God's own, just like me.* The notion gave me pause, but I kept on walking.

As I approached my car, that "still, small voice" inside me said: "I want you to give that woman some money." I was already 50 feet from the bakery. It was too late. I got into my car and headed for work.

As I drove into the parking lot of my work a couple minutes later, I was again prompted by the voice: "I want you to go give that woman some money." This time, the voice was more commanding than requesting. Commanding enough that I had to pay attention.

*OK,* I thought, *but I really have to hurry.*

I drove back to the store. Before I got out of the car, I pulled out my wallet, took out a five-dollar bill, rolled it neatly in the palm of my hand, and walked back into the store. The woman was still there, head in her hands, elbows on the table, with her face now totally hidden from view.

"Excuse me," I said. She either didn't hear me or chose to ignore me.

"Excuse me," I repeated.

She looked up as if to say, "What do you want?" I placed the money on the corner of her table. "What's this?" she asked angrily.

I was shocked and couldn't think of anything to say.

"Well, what is it? What do you want?"

I recovered quickly. "God told me to give you this.... I'm sorry if I offended you.... I'm just doing what God said to do." I thought she was going to throw it in my face.

Not knowing what else to do, I turned to make a hasty retreat from the store. I glanced back and saw that she was following me. I kept walking as fast as I could.

"Hey!" she yelled loudly enough for all those in the front of the store to hear. Briskly, I exited the store and began crossing the parking lot. "Hey, you!" I heard again. This time she was outside and I knew, if she so chose, she could scratch the side of my car as I made my hasty retreat.

I stopped dead in my tracks, assuming a defensive posture. I had no idea what to expect from her, but I was sure it would be some kind of attack.

"You gotta know this," she said as she came closer.

In retrospect, I'm amused at how I reacted to her approach. I pulled one arm up to my chest, ready to fend off any sudden blows, threw my head back, and firmly planted my feet. I was ready for anything.

"My mother died last week," she began, starting to cry. "I couldn't even afford to call home, much less go..." I began to relax my guard. "...and this morning, I didn't even have enough money to buy some food..." My heart went out to her. "...not even a donut..." I couldn't help feeling the fullness within myself, remembering how hungry I'd been just half an hour ago.

"I was sitting there, being really mad with God, and I told him in no uncertain terms, 'Why can't you take care of me the way you take care of other folks?' I was really mad. And about that time you come up with that little do-gooder smile on your face and say, 'Excuse me, excuse me.' I could've smacked you silly."

My defenses were alerted. It could still happen, I told myself. She laughed as though she could read my thoughts. "And then I saw that money," she said, softening her tone, smiling.

She began to cry again. "Well, I know now that God does take care of me.... He always has.... And I want to apologize ... to you and to him. And now," she said, taking a deep breath and smiling, "I'm gonna go have breakfast."

I got into my car, started it, adjusted the heating controls, and began to review the events of the morning. I had to stay in the parking lot for a few minutes. I couldn't see to drive because of the tears clouding my eyes.

I'd been so busy, I had actually resisted a "call" from God. Fortunately, I listened the second time.

*Angels are everyday wonders.
They are reminders to us that life is not
just what we see and touch, or what
we define and explain. Life is also
invisible friends and protectors
who stand by us to the end.*

For ages we have painted angels
on ceilings and canvases. For years
we have tried to capture their likenesses.
We must not forget to put as much effort
into understanding and recognizing
angels as we have put into
how we perceive them.

# Voice in the Storm

HE RAIN STARTED around six. I didn't think much
about it at the time. Mountain folks like me
are used to the brief thunderstorms that are a
common occurrence in the Colorado Rockies. Bob
had taken the kids into town to do some shopping
after supper. I relished the solitude. You don't get
much of it when you have three preschoolers.

Though there were dishes to wash and chores to
do, I curled up in the big comfy chair by the front
window that overlooks the Big
Thompson River. I'd been reading
a mystery novel and couldn't wait
to get back to it. I was soon so
engrossed that the intermittent
crashes of thunder and flashes of lightning
seemed like part of the story.

Darkness settled in early, and I got up
to turn on the lights. Then I glimpsed the
road through the driving rain; water was

rushing down it. I hoped Bob wasn't coming back through the storm. He'd have trouble seeing the yellow lines on the twisty narrow road. Flash floods, fed by mountain cloudbursts, occur from time to time in the mountains. Folks usually wait them out. I hoped that Bob would buy the kids an ice cream and hang around in town for a while.

I went back to my book, this time more to mask the concern I was feeling than to find out the story's murderer. I couldn't concentrate. *Perhaps,* I thought, *there would be some information about the storm on the radio.* When I got up to turn it on, I looked through the darkness at the river in front of me. It had risen some, but I was less worried about the river than the road. I fiddled with the dials looking for a local station that would have news of the storm. There wasn't much. The commentator mentioned high water, but there were no flood warnings yet.

I decided I might as well get the dishes done. There was no avoiding them, and work might keep my

mind off my family. I dreaded the
thought that they might be
driving up through "The
Narrows." Surely the road
would be covered with
water there, and driving
would be treacherous.

I still hadn't begun to worry about my own safety.
Our house, after all, was well above the river.

The phone rang, and I rushed to get it, hoping
it was Bob. I'd tell him to just stay the night with our
cousins in town. No sense risking getting stranded in
the car with three little kids.

It wasn't Bob. I recognized Kenny, our closest
neighbor downstream. It was the bridge in front of his
house that my family would have to cross to get to our
cabin. "It's giving way," he warned. "Don't try to go
over it."

Terrified by the implication of his words, I
explained that Bob might be approaching the bridge.

"I wouldn't worry," said Kenny. "I heard that the
sheriff's not letting anyone start up into the canyon.

Guess we're lucky not to live down by the bottom of the river. We'd be looking at a lot of water damage."

As I started to respond, the phone went dead and all the lights in the house went off. I opened the back-door to check for lights in neighboring houses. The world was inky black. The wind blew eerily. The angry river hissed.

Slamming the door shut, I moved hastily through the darkness to grab my coat and the flashlight. If Bob and the kids were already in the canyon, I knew I'd have to warn them not to use the bridge.

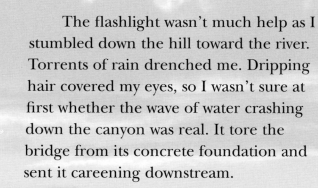

The flashlight wasn't much help as I stumbled down the hill toward the river. Torrents of rain drenched me. Dripping hair covered my eyes, so I wasn't sure at first whether the wave of water crashing down the canyon was real. It tore the bridge from its concrete foundation and sent it careening downstream.

I hurried back in the direction of the house. At least I'd be safe there. If Bob did try to come home, he'd see that the bridge was out.

Already I was cold. It would be good to be inside. I'd light the fire we always kept laid in the fireplace and warm up beside it.

I'd just reached the door when I heard a sound...a sound like a child sobbing. It came from above me on the hill. I listened intently. It wasn't the crying of any of my own little ones...a mom can tell her child's cry. I tried to persuade myself that it was an animal, perhaps a stranded bobcat. I wanted to get in out of the cold rain, but when the sound came again, I couldn't ignore it. What if a terrified toddler was really up there, lost and alone, in the pounding rain?

I began climbing slowly and carefully toward the spot where the sound seemed to have come. The jagged rocks were slippery and tore through my jeans when I fell. This is really foolish, I told myself. There can't be a child out here. I aimed my flashlight upward. Nothing! I was ready to turn back when I heard the crying sound again. I continued upward, until, utterly exhausted, I reached the top of the mountain behind our cabin.

The wind had abated slightly, and I no longer heard the crying. Maybe they were one and the same. I wasn't sure, but I was too tired to care. I did not dare climb down. I'd probably break a leg on the descent in the darkness. I shined the flashlight on my watch: 1:30 A.M. The rain would most certainly stop by morning, and I'd be able to see a way to get safely back to our house.

I huddled in a small niche in the boulders and slept intermittently. The sound of churning helicopter blades woke me. A rope ladder was being lowered through the murky sky above.

A man then motioned to me to climb it. Like an obedient child, I did. Strong hands pulled me into the chopper, and then the pilot lifted the helicopter. Voices couldn't be heard over the noise of the blades, so I couldn't ask why I'd been plucked from the mountain. But as soon as I looked down, I knew. The rampaging river had raced down the canyon, carrying with it everything in its path.

Trees and power lines had fallen prey to its force. Bridges and buildings were dragged downstream and deposited in jumbled masses. The helicopter hovered, and I looked in horror at the spot where our house had stood. Part of the chimney was all that remained. If I had been inside, I would have died in the devastation. I could only pray that my family had not come home after I headed up the mountain.

When the helicopter landed on the Loveland High School football field, I followed a Red Cross worker into the gym. People milled everywhere. A few large portable chalkboards listed the names of missing people. I saw mine. I didn't see Bob's or the children's. I breathed a sigh of relief. I was certain they must be safe.

As I stood figuring out how to contact him, Bob's strong arms encircled me. His eyes were moist. "Thank God you're safe. How did you know to get to higher ground?"

I told him about the crying I'd heard, and I reminded him of the Bible verse that says, "a little child shall lead you." I knew without a doubt that God had sent a little child to lead me.

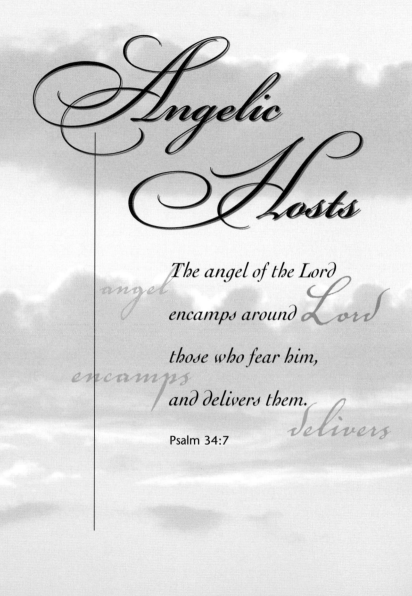

# Angelic Hosts

The angel of the Lord
encamps around
those who fear him,
and delivers them.

Psalm 34:7

# Angelic Acts of Kindness

HERE'S A FAMOUS line in the classic movie *A Streetcar Named Desire* that says, "I have always depended on the kindness of strangers." I've frequently quoted this line because it's been true for me.

The Bible speaks of "attending angels unaware" and guardian angels, but I have learned that "angels" are not always immortal beings from heaven. Because they are God's messengers, they can come in many forms. The dictionary says an angel can also be "a kind and lovable person." This is the kind of angel I've encountered often in my lifetime.

One time someone ran into my mailbox during the night. When I called the post office in the morning, I was told to also report it to the State Police. After the officer looked over the damage and wrote up a report, he mentioned that he would be off the next day and would stop by to "fix it up." I thought he  meant to put in some nails to hold the splintered wood together. But he arrived with a thick post, posthole digger, and cement for the base support. When the officer was finished, all he would accept for his generosity and hard work was a cup of coffee.

People have joked with me that my car is a nail magnet. I get two or three new tires every year. In fact, I've lost track of how many times a stranger has stopped to help me fix a flat tire, only to smile and wave away any notion of reward other than my genuine words of thanks.

Then there was the summer my lawn mower was broken. On more than one occasion, I came home from work to find my one-acre lawn newly mown, until my mower was fixed. One winter it snowed for several days and drifted too deep for me to get the car out of the yard.

I heard a loud motor sound in the yard and ran to the door to see a plow clearing my driveway. On its second pass the driver smiled, waved, and kept on going. The smile and wave seem to be trademarks of kind strangers. There are times when I've come home to find a dazzling basket of fresh vegetables sitting on my back step. There's never a note with the basket.

I live in the country, where we call each other "neighbors" even if we live ten miles apart and don't know each other's name. Sometimes we recognize a face or passing car without really knowing the person. But in a time of need, the stranger who's a neighbor becomes an angel through their kindness.

My most dramatic encounter happened on a cold, drizzly winter night. On my way to work in the morning, I noticed that the dashboard reading for my car's voltmeter indicated my battery was not charging. Since the battery was fairly new, I thought it might be a computer misread. I figured I would stop to get it checked on my way home from work.

That evening, riding on a busy three-lane highway, I noticed the car was steadily losing power but surged if nothing was running. I immediately turned off the lights, wipers, radio, and heater and rode down the shoulder with the flashers on. It was risky, but I only had another mile to go to get to the auto repair shop. I prayed the whole way: "Please just let me make it off the exit ramp and to the shop." As I coasted through the tollbooth, the car died.

Frustrated, I didn't know what to do. Just then a knock on my window startled me. It was the driver of the vehicle behind me. Amazingly, in this day of road rage, he had never honked or yelled. Instead, he was offering to push my car with his pickup and help me.

Once we steered out of the way, he popped the hood and checked it out. I was explaining to him how the car had acted, and he said it must have been the alternator that failed and that I had drained the battery of whatever stored charge it had left. He offered me a ride to the auto shop. When we got there, he told the circumstances to the mechanic and requested a loaner battery to get the car to the shop without being towed.

Once we got back to my car, it took another 45 minutes to rig up the other battery. Unfortunately, neither one of us had the appropriate tools for making the job easier. Somehow, despite the steady, icy drizzle and aggravating circumstances, the man never lost his temper.

When he finally got my car to run, he followed me back to the shop and squared things with the mechanic. Then he offered to drive me home. By now he had spent an hour and a half of his time with me and was soaked to the skin. His supper was probably drying out or cold by now. Even though I lived only a short distance away, I couldn't bring myself to let him do any more—I felt bad enough already. I didn't even have five dollars to offer him. I knew I could call someone to come get me, so I told him to go home and change his clothes.

I asked him if he was married, and he was. I patted him on the shoulder and said,

"Tell your wife not to be angry with you for being late. Tell her she's married to an angel because tonight you have been my guardian angel. God sent you to look out for me." Later, I thought I should at least send him a thank-you card, but I realized I hadn't found out his name, where he lived, or where he worked.

Sometimes we hear people speak of "what goes around comes around." They often say it in a negative way, referring to someone who's mean or done something spiteful, implying they will "get theirs" someday. For every negative, however, there's a positive. I believe that for every act of kindness, every smile we send out, another will return to us. Kindness has that sort of boomerang effect.

All the people I've mentioned—and the many I didn't have room to include—are the true epitome of angels. They offer their kindness without any thought of reward. They do good deeds because for them it seems like the right thing to do. For all my angels, I pray God will bless them a thousand times in return just as he has blessed me by sending them into my life. I've depended on their kindness, and they have never let me down.

# Gift-Giving Ripples

ON CHRISTMAS EVE, a message was left on Hope's answering machine: "My name is Merlene. I have a package here that I think belongs to you. Please give me a call." She then left her number.

That evening, Hope telephoned Merlene, who explained that a package had come to her mailbox by mistake. She said she could barely read the name on the label, but with the help of a magnifying glass, and by looking in the phone book, she believed she had found the rightful owner.

Hope and her husband, Bertram, arranged to pick up the errant package that evening. They knew their daughter, Alison, would be relieved to hear they had finally received it.

They located Merlene in a vintage apartment complex. Hope waited in the car while Bertram went to get the package. Merlene, a pleasant, comely woman in her forties, introduced herself and her ten-year-old son, Jonathan.

"We apologize for opening the box. My son and the boy I babysit opened it, thinking it was ours." Merlene had put everything neatly back into the carton and resealed it.

Bertram glanced around the tidy room; he noted the well-worn rug and sofa and the dimly lit lamp in the corner, but he saw no sign of Christmas.

"We won't be having a Christmas this year," Merlene told him, as if reading Bertram's mind. "My son and I have been in a financial crunch lately, so we're forgoing a Christmas tree and gifts this year."

Alison always sent beautiful gifts, purchased from an upscale department store, so that Hope and Bertram could exchange them, if needed. Bertram knew that Merlene could have kept the package and returned the merchandise for cash.

With many thanks, Bertram put the package under his arm and went out to the car. Merlene followed him out to meet Hope and say good-bye. Before pulling away, Bertram got out of the car, pressed something into Merlene's hand and closed her fingers over it. He quickly got back into the car, put up the window while waving good-bye, and drove away.

Later that evening, Hope phoned her sister, Nancy, in California and told her about the incident. As Nancy listened, she felt moved to do something for Merlene and her son.

Nancy wrote to Merlene using the sketchy information that Hope had given her. Hope knew only Merlene's first name and part of an address. With a prayer in her heart, Nancy wrote:

"Dear Merlene,

We haven't met, but you've met my sister and her husband when a package destined for them was mistakenly delivered to your house. Hearing Hope's story of your honesty touched our hearts! So, in the spirit of giving, we'd like to spread Christmas around to more than our family. Please take this token of money and use it as you see fit. God has blessed us, and we want to share his goodness with you and your son. God bless you.

Nancy and Joe Denson."

Merlene did receive Nancy's letter, and she promptly responded:

"Dear Nancy and Joe,

How wonderful are the Lord's blessings, and how mysterious are his ways. I am a single parent of a ten-year-old son. I've been trying the best I can to tell him that honesty is always the best policy, no matter what. Not because of any earthly rewards, but because it's the honorable way. It's amazing how far the story of this little act of honesty has gone and the blessings it has brought. My son and I live in a neighborhood where acts of kindness aren't usually appreciated. Not even with a simple 'thank you.' My son says, 'Why do things for other people, then?' I simply think it's the right thing to do.

Your letter and gift are helping my son realize that while we sure didn't expect a reward for our actions, sometimes the Lord uses others to help provide blessings. Your dollars went immediately to the grocery store. Thank you for your generosity and the memories we now have because of it. I guess the Lord really is listening and knows our needs.

May your New Year be filled with a new closeness to our Lord and Savior. God Bless.

Sincerely, Merlene and Jonathan."

This story of giving does not end here. Since that Christmas exchange, other family members have written notes and given gifts of encouragement to Merlene and Jonathan. Alison's fiancé was deeply touched by this episode and sent Merlene a gift, as did Nancy's children, sisters, brother, and other members of the family.

In a later letter, Merlene wrote, "I am not as discouraged as I was a few months back. When I think of the Christmas package and finding the true owners, it seems so small and insignificant compared to what you and your family have done for me and my son. I can see only a small portion of the picture, where thankfully God sees the whole picture."

Our family determined that the next Christmas would be different. Gift-giving would include Merlene and Jonathan, as well as other people like them. Just like throwing a pebble into a pond, the ripples keep spreading ever outward.

*Who are these godly beings that minister to us?*
*They are wise and wonderful personalities that come*
*before us in visions, in dreams, and in person.*

# My Prison Camp Vow

by Corrie ten Boom
(as told to Muriel Larson)

I WAS IN MOSCOW. The customs officer was ransacking the suitcase of the person ahead of me. "Oh, Heavenly Father," I prayed, "what will happen when he finds all those Bibles in my suitcase? Will he send me back to Holland, or even to prison?" At that time the Communist dictatorship was still in power. Vivid memories of those horrible days I spent in a German concentration camp during World War II flashed into my mind.

Bowing my head, I prayed, "Lord, you said in Jeremiah 1, 'I will hasten my word to perform it.' Well, I claim that promise. These Bibles in my suitcase are your Word. Now, Lord, please watch over these Bibles I'm smuggling in!"

I raised my eyes to the suitcase. Beings of light surrounded it—angels! Then they vanished before my eyes, and my fears disappeared, too.

When my turn came with the customs officer, he picked up my suitcase. "That's a heavy one!" he exclaimed. "Let me carry it to your car for you."

I could hardly keep from shouting, "Hallelujah!"

This was only one of the many times I have seen the Lord's hand in my life as I've sought to bring his message of salvation, love, provision, and power to needy souls all over the world. I communicated especially well with prisoners because I was one myself in one of the most notorious of the Nazi concentration camps—Ravensbruck.

No, I was not a Jew. I was sent there because I had participated in an organization in Haarlem, Holland, that helped many Jewish people escape torture and death at the hands of the Nazis. And I would certainly do it again.

At the age of five, I came to know the Lord Jesus Christ as my personal Savior. Even at that early age I had a deep desire to see others also come to know him. In fact, I prayed that everyone in my neighborhood would be saved. One part of that prayer was to be answered 73 years later!

Although my brother Willem and sister Nollie had married, my sister Betsie and I never did. We stayed with our father in our home and helped him in his watch shop. I became the first licensed woman watchmaker in Holland. I also had the joy of teaching the Bible in many schools and churches and starting Christian clubs for girls through which many came to receive Jesus as their Savior.

In 1940, the Nazi hordes came down upon us. As time went on, harassment of the Jews increased until they began to disappear. Then one day four German soldiers raided the fur shop of our neighbor, Mr. Weil.

He watched helplessly as they broke glass and carried out armloads of furs.

Betsie and I ran to Mr. Weil. "Come with us, quick!" I gasped. We brought him to our home.

"What can we do to save him?" Betsie wondered aloud.

"Willem!" I exclaimed. Our minister brother had rescued other Jews. He would know what to do. I traveled by train to Hilversum, where Willem lived. He wasn't there, so I told his wife and their grown son, Kik.

"Tell Mr. Weil to be ready as soon as it's dark," Kik said. That night he came to our home and led Mr. Weil away to safety.

Two weeks later I saw Kik again. "What happened to Mr. Weil?" I asked.

He smiled at me. "If you're going to work with the underground, Tante Corrie, you must learn not to ask questions."

After that, a trickle, then a stream of Jews came to our door seeking refuge and help. Before I knew it, I was in charge of a major operation to save the Jews, and our home was the headquarters! A beautifully camouflaged secret room was built into my bedroom.

The time came, however, when we couldn't smuggle the Jews out of the country or find them places to stay. Before long we had seven fugitives staying with us.

One day when I was sick with fever, the Nazis raided our house. Our Jewish friends scurried into the concealed chamber, but the Nazis took my father, brother, sisters, nephew, and me to the Scheveningen prison. We were all separated from one another.

Because of my illness, I was put into solitary confinement for four months. During that time I learned that my sister Nollie, brother Willem, and nephew had been released, but the imprisonment had been too harsh for my elderly father's frail body. He had gone to be with the Lord. Betsie and I were still held.

While I was in solitary confinement, I entered into a deeper experience with my Lord, and I knew that his everlasting arms were around me. What a precious experience!

I was called before the man who would decide whether I would live or be shot. He questioned me about my activities, which led me to tell about my work with the feebleminded.

"What a waste of time and energy!" he exclaimed.

"Sir, if you knew Jesus, you should know he has a great love for everyone who is despised," I said.

"Guard!" he shouted. "Take this woman back to her cell."

The next morning he called me back. "I could not sleep last night thinking about what you said," he admitted. "Tell me more about Jesus."

And so I did. Betsie also witnessed to this lieutenant. After that, he did everything in his power to protect us, but we were sent from there to Vught and from there to the most notorious women's extermination camp in Germany, Ravensbruck, where 97,000 women were killed or died. There God used Betsie and me to bring to Jesus many who were doomed to death.

Betsie always praised the Lord for everything, even for the lice that kept the guards away from our barracks so that we could hold services every night. The whole atmosphere of our crowded barracks changed while we were there, from one of cursing and ill will to one of love and thoughtfulness.

One night Betsie wakened me. "Corrie," she said, "God has spoken to me. When we are free, we must bring the gospel to people around the world. The Lord will give us strength, help, and money. We can tell from experience that Jesus' light is stronger than the deepest darkness."

"All right, Betsie, we will," I vowed. A week later Betsie died from disease and starvation. And a week after her death, I was released.

After that God sent me to proclaim the gospel to people all over the world. Billy Graham gave me the privilege of testifying to millions who viewed his crusade on television. After I spoke on a popular television program in Holland, I learned that a neighbor for whom I had prayed when I was five had come to Christ that night—73 years later!

Through my books Betsie's testimony also went out to the world, just as God had said it would.

*May you always walk with the morning star to guide you, the summer sun on your back, and an angel by your side.*

# Compound Interest

EW PEOPLE EVER suspected that Sue Ellen had a problem. She juggled her roles as wife to Phil, mother to Harlan and Katy, and her at-home job as a writer so successfully that people called her a regular Martha Stewart. But in time, everyone knew.

"It's not a problem," Sue Ellen had said when her husband sat her down one evening and asked her about her drinking. "Maybe I have been having a few more drinks lately," she admitted, "but life's been kind of hectic, what with the move, Dad's heart attack, and all the time you've had to spend traveling for work. Besides," she'd continued defensively, "I can stop any time I want to. Remember last year, I didn't have a single drink during Lent."

Phil had patted her arm. He'd put off talking to Sue Ellen about the problem for months, maybe years.

He loved her despite her drinking and had truly hoped that this moment of reckoning would never come. "Honey," he said, "I'm just worried about you. Tell you what, we just won't keep any liquor in the house. Then you won't be tempted." When Sue Ellen frowned at him, he added tenderly, "I'm not trying to be mean. I'm only doing it because I love you."

Sue Ellen hadn't said anything. She knew it wouldn't be hard to stow away a bottle or two for those times when she really needed a drink.

At Sue Ellen's annual checkup, the doctor had noticed the shaking hands and weight loss—signs of alcoholism. He had asked her about her drinking. "Alcohol can cause liver damage," he'd said. "These pamphlets discuss the dangers of excessive drinking and give you the numbers of a local AA contact."

Sue Ellen had politely thanked him for the literature but protested, "Don't worry about me, I just drink socially. I certainly don't have a drinking problem."

A few months later, Harlan's preschool teacher asked Sue Ellen to stay for a few minutes after class. Mrs. Murphy had waited until all the other parents left. She'd sent Harlan across the hall on an errand and then asked Sue Ellen to sit down. "It's about the field trip to the farm," she'd said. "I know you volunteered to be a driver, but several of the other mothers have told me that they don't want their children riding in your car. When the moms have chatted with you in the hall, they've noticed that you've smelled like you'd been drinking."

Sue Ellen had been offended.

"I'm only mentioning this because we all care about you," said Mrs. Murphy. "And, of course, we care about the welfare of the children, so we can't let you drive for field trips until you stop drinking."

"It's really none of their business," said Sue Ellen. "Besides I hardly ever drink in the daytime."

"One of our other mothers is in AA," said Mrs. Murphy. "I know she'd be happy to talk with you."

Sue Ellen had declined the offer. She'd also adamantly declined her mother's offer to come and stay with the children so Sue Ellen could go to a residential treatment facility.

"We're worried about you, dear," her mother said. "Sometimes your words seem a little slurred when we call."

"It's just my allergies," Sue Ellen had reassured her.

On a day the kids didn't have school, Sue Ellen called the mother of one of Katy's friends. "We'd love to have Rachel come over to play."

"I'm sorry, Sue Ellen, but we don't feel you are able to provide adequate supervision when you've been drinking. We'd love to have Katy come here, though."

Sputtering furiously, Sue Ellen had slammed down the phone. "Rachel's mom says you can play there," she'd explained to Katy.

When Katy left, Sue Ellen fixed herself a glass of gin and sat down in the rocker in the living room. She was still there a little later when the doorbell rang. She started to stand to get the door but, being a little unsteady, just called out, "Come on in."

It was Katy's teacher. "What a surprise!" said Sue Ellen. She hadn't said it was a pleasant surprise, because it wasn't. *Maybe,* she thought, *Ms. Steffens would think the gin was just ice water.*

Ms. Steffens wasn't fooled. She didn't beat around the bush either.

"I've come here today because I'm worried about Katy. The other children are beginning to talk about your drinking problem, and I'm afraid that soon other mothers won't want their children playing with her if your drinking continues."

Suddenly Sue Ellen was sobbing. "It's already happened. Just today Rachel's mother said she couldn't come over here."

Ms. Steffens spoke soothingly, "I know you love your little ones, and you want the best for them. Your drinking is not something you can control yourself. I have a friend in AA. Would you like her to come over?"

Sue Ellen hesitated only a second. "Yes," she said firmly.

Six months later, still sober, Sue
Ellen went to school to thank Ms.
Steffens. She hugged the older woman and said, "You were an angel to help me face my drinking problem."

Ms. Steffens smiled and said, "I was just one of the many angels sent to encourage you to seek help. Sometimes it takes a whole heavenly host to get God's message across."

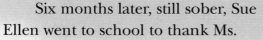

# Angels in a Korean Orphanage

WAS IN A hurry to leave the Korean orphanage on the outskirts of Seoul that December day in 1951. I had seen enough of what war can do to children. It takes away their families. Burns their innocent faces. Leaves them without eyes, arms, legs. And gives them horrible memories that will linger forever in their dreams.

I wanted to get through Seoul before dark. It was bad enough in the daytime with all the narrow, cluttered streets and the drivers veering out in front of other vehicles with no warning. If we could beat nightfall, I would not have to drive the 50-odd miles on dirt roads with those amber blackout lights all military vehicles have. I was anxious to go.

But the chaplain to whom I was assigned as an assistant was in no hurry to leave. I knew he was concerned about the children, because he had tried to speak to each of them,  fighting back tears as he saw their mangled limbs and scarred faces. He was sad knowing we wouldn't be coming back to the orphanage again; our division was being transferred to Japan in less than a month.

Just as the chaplain was beginning to say some last good-byes, a young woman ran into the room talking and gesturing excitedly. "She wants us to stay a while longer," Lee, our interpreter, translated. "The children have something for us."

*Oh, no!* I thought. *We'll never make it back to the outfit before dark.*

The chaplain had heard of the orphanage from a Presbyterian missionary. Some of the Korean Christians—Methodists, Presbyterians, and Catholics— had obtained an abandoned school facility and converted it into a makeshift home for war orphans. We took several boxes of clothes sent over by the chaplain's church in the states and a few hundred dollars contributed by the troops. The children were afraid of us at first; they associated uniforms with shells, bullets, planes, and napalm fires. But Lee told them we were like the missionaries and had come to help them. Soon they were crowding around us, tugging at our field jackets and bowing when we emptied our pockets of C-ration chocolate bars and chewing gum.

After we had unloaded the clothes and the chaplain presented the money to the man in charge, we were given a tour of the orphanage. We walked through the sleeping quarters, which consisted of mats on a clean floor, and we saw a kitchen that contained a few black pots for cooking rice and rows of little wooden eating bowls with chopsticks. The "stove" was actually a fire in a hole at the rear of the building. In the makeshift infirmary, volunteer surgeons and nurses treated the wounded. Seeing the scarred faces, crooked limbs, crutches, bandages, eye patches, burns, and scars, the chaplain broke into tears.

So many questions nagged at me. Why does God allow wars to happen, robbing little children of their parents and homes? If Jesus loves the little children, why does he permit them to suffer like this? And why were we here in the first place? Had our shells, bombs, and napalm wounded some of these children?

I was startled from my thoughts when the young woman came rushing through the door. "She wants us to wait," Lee said. "The children have been practicing." Then, on cue from the woman, about 20 children began to take their places in a choir formation. A young man brought three old chairs for us to sit on.

The children began to sing "Savior, Like a Shepherd Lead Us" in beautiful cherubic harmony. I quickly forgot my nagging questions and doubts. There was hope in their voices—the freshness of youth, the promise of laughter, of love, and of faith.

And their singing held intimations of better days—the love of their caretakers, companionship of their peers, a time of peace, and trust in the Jesus they were praising in song.

Teary-eyed, the chaplain stood and removed his helmet. I did likewise. Both of us realized we had been given a momentary glimpse of the Kingdom of God by the one who had promised it to little children. All we could do was stand in reverent silence as if in the presence of angels.

*Angels are the unseen hands that applaud you and the heavenly voices that cheer you on. All you have to do is listen and look with your heart.*

# Gathering of Angels in Jellico

**S**IRENS WAILED IN the night, echoing through the community of Jellico, Tennessee. Flames crackled and roared, leaping far into the dark sky, casting flickering shadows across the scene of devastation. Yet another church had been destroyed by flames, swelling the list of church-burnings that had occurred throughout the nation. There wasn't much anyone could do. The small building crumbled and collapsed, completely burned to the ground.

It wasn't the first church to burn. It wouldn't be the last. But for the close-knit African-American congregation of the First Baptist Church of Jellico, it was their only church, and losing it hurt them all. Their little church had been there a long time, and now it was gone.

They joined forces to start all over again, knowing the work would be hard and lengthy. Some of the parishioners borrowed on their homes to help out, and many worked with their own hands to help rebuild what flames had so swiftly destroyed. But the work progressed slowly. Gradually, the frame and the roof went up, and the congregation rejoiced. But there were still no bathrooms, no plumbing, and no interior walls. So much hard work lay before them.

Meanwhile, in another state, Tom and Mary Hayden had been watching the nightly news, which was mostly bad news, as usual. Over the years they had seen too much footage of devastation and destruction, watching clip after clip of churches burned to the ground through the flames of ignorance. Tom hated seeing so many decent people left with smoldering ruins where once they had worshipped together. He'd had enough!

Mary turned to him as they watched and asked, "What are you going to do about it?"

What, indeed? What could one person do? He knew he couldn't stop the church burnings. He couldn't change the news reports. He could not change hearts that were filled with hate and bigotry. But he had to do something, and so he began calling around in search of something he could do to make a difference. He soon found Jellico, with its small, faithful congregation, working away at restoring their church. Tom contacted Pastor Gerald Littlejohn, and thus the Nehemiah Project began.

As often as he could, Tom drove the two hours to Jellico. He brought hammers, nails, and whatever tools he could find, and he brought as many helpers as he could round up, too. All kinds of people helped out, giving up their weekend plans to work long hours on the new church building. They constructed the stage where the minister would speak each Sunday. They hired experts to do the bulldozing and bricklaying. They worked on insulation. They put up walls and set new floors.

Every month Tom gathered his work crew. They were not always the same people, but there were always enough for a couple teams. They came from many different backgrounds and from different churches and beliefs. They worked in a wide variety of professions—there were salespeople, students, professors, engineers, doctors, computer programmers, and others. Tom brought his own plumber to help out, and a retired carpenter pitched in to donate his expertise. A full-time builder showed up with his own group of 15 assistants.

Campus Crusade for Christ sent a group of volunteers. A pastor from Columbia, visiting the United States for a while, also showed up to help. A couple missionaries on home leave drove down. One young student wanted to help, so she went out and bought herself a brand-new hammer and joined the work crews. Men from a university football team were also anxious to do their part.

Everyone took turns bringing food. And the congregation in Jellico joined the volunteers for meals and a visit, eating, singing, and praying together after they did their work.

Not everyone understood Tom's Nehemiah Project at first. Some people couldn't quite make sense of his desire to reach out to others no matter who or where those "others" might be. Not everyone felt friendly at first, and a few people were downright suspicious. Some of Jellico's residents looked at Tom and his friends as upper-class do-gooders who would perform a moment of charity in order to believe they were good people and then return to their nice, comfortable homes and lives. After a while, however, attitudes visibly changed. Resistance melted away as, month after month, Tom and his workers faithfully drove two hours to get there, worked all day, then wearily headed home again.

Perhaps Tom's project touched hearts and set an example of what people can do for one another if they care and want to make a difference. Tom named his project for the book of Nehemiah, thinking of

chapter 2, verse 17 (NIV): "...its gates have been burned with fire. Come, let us rebuild...." That's what Tom and his helpers did, counting on chapter 6, verse 9 (KJV): "Now therefore, O God, strengthen my hands."

The work was hard and required long hours. But perhaps Tom understood that the ultimate goal was not just to rebuild a church that had burned down. The Nehemiah Project also helped build a bridge between people, between hearts, and between spirits. Together, they built something no fire could ever destroy.

*When we are in touch with the angels,*
*we walk to a heavenly rhythm*
*that guides our way.*

# Tan Van

BOLTED UPRIGHT FROM my bed, startled from my sleep and wideawake with dream images still vivid in my mind. The dark night surrounded me in silence, and I felt my heart pounding wildly. In the dream I'd been driving along, everything fine and ordinary, when suddenly a tan-colored van burst from a side road, cutting me off. I woke with a sense of screeching tires and metal crunching as the van and my car collided. I knew the wreck had been serious, very serious. I felt as shaken as if the accident had actually happened.

The dream felt so real, so terrifying, so urgent, somehow unlike any other dream. I got off my bed and paced the house for several minutes. I felt so shaken and so vulnerable. But it was late. I was weary and soon dropped back into bed and slept. No more dreams disturbed my night.

By morning, I had forgotten the dream. I didn't remember even being awake during the night. My mind hummed with chores to do, places to go, and problems to deal with. The day shaped up as crammed full and busy as every other day. Nothing unusual or odd. If I even recalled dreaming, I probably would have laughed at my irrational fearfulness about it. Just a dream, that's all.

I hopped into my car to drive my son and his friends off to school. No problem. We chatted, laughed, and made plans. Everything went along smoothly. In fact, there was less traffic than usual. No jams, no careless drivers stuck to my back bumper, no close calls. I never felt a moment of uneasiness. The dream was long gone, and I had totally forgotten it.

On the way home after dropping the boys at school, my mind was preoccupied with tasks that needed to be done. My day moved along steadily, absolutely normal. Only several hours later, when I left the house again for an errand, suddenly I felt odd. I felt uneasy for no apparent reason. I checked to be sure my seat belt was snug and made sure I had plenty of gas, those sorts of things. But I had no idea what caused this uneasy feeling.

Then, as if someone sat beside me in the car, nudging me to remember, the dream leapt into my mind. My heart pounded wildly in my chest. I remembered how vivid the dream had felt—how very real. I'd never had a dream before that left me as shaken. How could I have forgotten that strange dream? It wasn't like any other dream. It was as if someone had opened a window into the future and let me glimpse that frightening scene as a warning.

I slowed the car. My mind became a thousand times more alert. Perhaps it was only a stupid dream. Perhaps it meant nothing. But why had it suddenly come back to my mind? Why had I suddenly remembered it just as I was driving along a familiar street on a normal day? It also hit me that in the dream, I'd been alone in the car. My son and his friends hadn't been with me. Maybe that's why I hadn't remembered it earlier.

I'd never been as cautious as I was in that moment. So, when I swung the car around a blind curve, I was driving slower than usual, my foot ready to brake. Otherwise, I never could have stopped in time and have avoided the vehicle that darted out from the left, directly into the path of my car. I heard my brakes screech as I slammed down my foot with all my strength.

The other driver kept right on going. I pulled over to the side, breathing hard. I couldn't recall ever coming that close to a serious collision. Sure, there'd been fender benders now and then, but nothing like this would have been. My heart pounded. I felt a sense of shock and awe. If I hadn't felt the presence of someone tapping my shoulder to remind me of that dream, I'm sure I would have been involved in a dreadful wreck.

I felt a certainty in that moment. God's angels had been watching over me, sending a vivid dream, reminding me to be ready. I knew a guardian angel lingered by my side that seemingly ordinary day while

I went about my normal chores. My heart eventually slowed and calmed. My hands quit shaking, so I could continue driving. Later, when I told my family, their first question, of course, was "Mom, what color was the car that cut you off?"

"It wasn't a car," I told them.

They stared at me, puzzled, wondering what I meant. It was, of course, a tan van.

*For God so loves us, his children,
that he sent a heavenly host of angels
to guide, protect, and inspire us.*

# Passing It On

IT WAS DECEMBER 23, 1993. For a single mom who was going to college and supporting children completely alone, Christmas was looking bleak. I surveyed my little home, realization dawning like a slow, twisting pain. We were poor.

Our tiny house had two bedrooms, both off the living room. They were so small that my baby daughter's crib barely fit into one room, and my son's twin bed and dresser were squeezed against each other. There was no way they could share a room, so I made my bed every night on the living room floor. The three of us shared the only closet in the house. We were snug, always only a few feet from each other, day and night. With no doors on the children's rooms, I could see and hear them at all times. It made them feel secure, and it made me feel close to them—a blessing I wouldn't have had in other circumstances.

It was early evening, about 7:00. The snow was falling softly, silently, and my children were both asleep. I was wrapped in a blanket, sitting at the window, watching the powdery flakes flutter in the dimming light when my front door vibrated from a pounding fist.

Alarmed, I wondered who would stop by unannounced on such a snowy winter night. I opened the door to find a group of strangers, each grinning from ear to ear, their arms laden with boxes and bags.

Confused, but finding their joyous spirit contagious, I grinned right back.

"Are you Susan?" The man stepped forward as he held out a box for me.

Nodding stupidly, unable to find my voice, I was sure they thought I was mentally deficient.

"These are for you." The woman thrust another box at me with a huge, beaming smile. The porch light and the snow falling behind her cast a glow on her dark hair, lending her an angelic appearance.

I looked down into her box. It was filled to the top with delicious treats, a fat turkey, and all the makings of a traditional Christmas dinner. My eyes filled with tears as I realized why those people were there.

Finally coming to my senses, I found my voice and invited them in. Following her husband were two children, staggering with the weight of their packages. The family introduced themselves to me and told me their packages were all gifts for my little family. This wonderful, beautiful family, who were total strangers to me, somehow knew exactly what we needed. They brought wrapped gifts for each of us, a full buffet for me to make on Christmas day, and many "extras" that I could never afford. Visions of a beautiful, "normal" Christmas literally danced in my head. Somehow my secret wish for Christmas was materializing right in front of me. The desperate prayers of a single mom had been heard, and I knew right then that God had sent his angels my way.

My mysterious angels then handed me a white envelope, gave me another round of grins, and took turns hugging me. They wished me a Merry Christmas and disappeared into the night as suddenly as they had appeared.

Amazed and deeply touched, I looked around me at the boxes and gifts strewn at my feet and felt the ache of depression suddenly being transformed into a child-like joy. I began to cry, sobbing tears of the deepest gratitude. A great sense of peace filled me. The knowledge of God's love reaching into my tiny corner of the world enveloped me like a warm quilt. My heart was full. I fell to my knees amid all the boxes and offered a heartfelt prayer of thanks.

Getting to my feet, I wrapped myself in my blanket and sat once again to gaze out the window at the gently falling snow. Suddenly, I remembered the envelope. Like a child I ripped it open and gasped at what I saw. A shower of bills flitted to the floor. Gathering them up, I began to count all the five-, ten-, and twenty-dollar bills. As my vision blurred with tears, I counted the money, then counted it again to make sure I had it right. Sobbing again, I said it out loud: "One hundred dollars."

Even though my "angels" had showered me with gifts, they had somehow understood how desperately money was needed, too. There was no way they could have known it, but I had just received a disconnection notice from the gas company. I simply didn't have the money I needed, and I feared my family would be without heat by Christmas. The envelope of cash would give us warmth, as well as a tree for Christmas. Suddenly, we had all we needed and more.

I looked at my children sleeping soundly, and through my tears I smiled my first happy, free-of-worry smile in a long time. My smile turned into a grin as I thought about tomorrow: Christmas Eve. One visit from complete strangers had magically turned a painful day into a special one that we would always remember...with happiness.

It is now several years since our Christmas angels visited. I have remarried, and our household is happy and richly blessed. Every year since that Christmas in 1993, we have chosen a family less blessed than we are. We take them carefully selected gifts, food and treats, and as much money as we can spare. It's our way of passing on what was given to us. We hope that the cycle continues and that, someday, the families we share with will be able to pass it on, too.

Wherever my angels are, I thank you, and so do many other families. Without realizing how much, you have touched many lives. God bless you and all the Christmas angels out there.

*The presence of an angel is like a snowflake lightly touching you with its special gift, then evaporating into your warmth as you hurry on your way.*

*We can learn much more from angels about goodness and light than we will ever learn from this incandescent world in which we exist.*

# Angelic Keepsakes

Suddenly an angel of

the Lord appeared

and a light shone.

Acts 12:7

# A Special Photo of Joltin' Joe

"BEE-YER, GETCHA ICE-COLD beer!" The shouts echoed through Yankee Stadium. The scents of peanuts, popcorn, hot dogs, and a zillion other smells wafted along with the warm summer breeze as the crowd stood and roared expectantly. There was long, lean, Joltin' Joe DiMaggio, stepping up to the plate. He was an unlikely hero for a demure little girl like me. But I hadn't a clue back then just how much of a hero Joe was going to be—for my son and my entire family.

Years later, my 14-year-old son Larry, the second of seven children, was an honor student, hometown baseball star, and an avid collector of baseball memorabilia. The game ruled his life, and everyone just

knew this kid was going
to make it to the majors.
No doubt about it.

We were a baseball family back
then. Three or four evenings a week, plus
weekends, we'd all rush through an early
dinner and head out to the ballpark for games or
practice. Life was hectic but grand.

An industrious boy, Larry took a job that summer
to earn a little extra spending money. One particular
goal he achieved, after charming me out of my moth-
erly objections, was the purchase of a ten-speed bike.
He persuaded me that our Connecticut hills required
all those speeds. I took his rationalizations about my
fears and concerns with the proverbial grain of salt,
but, as usual, I caved. He seemed so strong—so inde-
structible.

One afternoon, Larry took off on his beloved
bike to go for a quick swim before work. He never had
that swim. He never arrived at work.

Coming down a hilly, curving road, Larry and the
bike suddenly hit a patch of sand. The bike stopped.

Larry didn't. He sailed through the air, plummeted down a ravine, and hit a tree trunk face-first.

Every blessed bone in his face, including the roof of his mouth, was broken, as well as each bone in his skull. Helmets for cyclists were unheard of back then.

A month or so later, after several surgeries, our boy came home. He walked into the house—a tall, bald, disfigured skeleton—went into his room, and shut the door. Our family's collective heart broke as the days and weeks went by. Other than visits to various doctors, Larry never ventured out; no school chums were allowed in. We tried to engage him—oh, how we tried—but nothing worked.

The neurosurgeon told Larry, "No more contact sports, son, other than baseball, that is." I was horrified, but the doctor wisely explained that, although ball-playing might be dangerous for Larry, to take away that part of his life could be worse.

Time passed, and I soon found myself wanting him to play ball as, box by box and folder by folder, Larry's baseball treasures came out of his room. "Throw these away," he'd mumble through wired jaws, "I don't need them anymore." I took them, but didn't throw them away, hoping he'd eventually change his mind.

Late one afternoon, a close neighbor came by to visit our reclusive son. As the father of Larry's best friend, Russ passed muster and was allowed into Larry's increasingly private sanctuary. A short while later, Larry came bounding down the hall. "Mom! Dad!" he called excitedly. "Look at this, will ya!" He held up a large, inscribed photograph of Joe DiMaggio. "I gotta show this to Jimmy and Mike!" With that, he dashed out of the house and ran over the hill to find his buddies.

Bewildered at the sudden turn of events, I looked at Russ with raised eyebrows. We sat down, and Russ, a private jet pilot for a business magnate, explained about his latest flight. His only passenger that day had been one of the businessman's friends...Joe DiMaggio.

During the flight, Russ told the famous center fielder all about our son. After landing, and while still on the tarmac, Joe stopped, opened his briefcase, and handed Russ a photograph of himself with the inscription, "To my pal Larry. Hang in there, kid. You can do it." Russ noticed a single tear roll down Joe's face.

One compassionate droplet for an unknown boy's hopes and dreams—just one kind moment in a famous athlete's busy life generated a truly glorious rebirth for our child.

Once out of his dark shell, Larry went on to play baseball and attend college, and he is now married with children of his own. That photograph of Joe still hangs on Larry's bedroom wall and smiles down at him every night. And every night, Larry smiles back.

Godspeed, Joe.

# A Teddy Bear Named Timothy

ON A COLD December day in 1997, my youngest son, Lance, and I headed to the mall. I wanted to get my holiday shopping out of the way. In fact, I wished the holidays themselves would just end. Ever since my second-eldest son, Timothy, had died, it had been hard for me to feel much joy, and Christmas only made it worse. Although I felt his absence every day, not having him there to open presents, frost cookies, or decorate the tree was especially depressing. I wished that I could somehow move past my grief, but so far that had proved impossible.

Lance and I meandered into a clothing store and headed in separate directions. As I was looking through the scarves, I heard someone say, "Can I help you?" I turned around and saw a sweetly smiling teenage boy.

"Have you seen my friend Bob?" he asked, holding out a sweater-adorned teddy bear. "His friend Billy just found a home, but he's got lots of other friends, if you're interested in adopting one of them."

I chuckled, suddenly noticing that the bears were strategically placed throughout the store. The young man walked on to chat with other customers, and I continued to browse.

When Lance and I had decided on our purchases, we headed up to the register. The boyish salesclerk had sold me on the teddy bears, so I decided to get one for myself. The salesgirl turned to the shelves behind her, filled with lonely bears, and asked if I wanted one with a green or blue sweater. When I said "green," she snatched one from the mass and plopped him down on the counter. But just before she rang him up, another salesgirl shouted, "Wait!" She reached behind the counter and pulled out a bear that she had adopted as her own. "Take this one," she said, smiling. "I've been taking care of him, but he needs a good home." I smiled back as I nodded my approval. It seemed fitting and sweet, as if I really would be taking care of him for her. Lance and I gathered our bags and headed back out into the mall.

"What's the bear's name?" my son asked.

I reached into the shopping bag and pulled out the bear. My heart sank as soon as I saw his name: Timothy.

*No, it couldn't be,* I thought. Not the name of all my emotions. Not the name that's been attached to so many joys and sorrows. I had to sit down.

As I wept, I came to a realization. I knew that no matter what, no matter when or where, my beloved son Timothy would always be with me, would always be in my heart. Tim hadn't disappeared into oblivion—he was up in heaven, watching and loving me, together with the Lord. Somehow, those thoughts made me feel better. I knew this wouldn't be the end of my pain—it would never go away completely. But for the first time in a long time, my heart seemed a little lighter, and I actually felt a sense of joy.

I grabbed the teddy bear and my son and held them tight. Then I put the bear in the bag, wiped the tears from my eyes, and stood up. I was ready to move on.

*Heavenly ears hear you and rush to touch you with love.*

*Angels can come to us in many ways,*
*in many shapes and sizes,*
*in laughter and tears,*
*in happiness as well as sorrow.*
*Angels are here with us in every part of life,*
*helping us, loving us, helping us to love.*

# Madge's Angelic Figurines

OUR FAMILY HAS always cherished Grandma Madge. She was a special lady with a knack for helping friends and family members when they needed it. Madge was always the first person to take a home-cooked meal to someone who was sick. The treasured time she spent with them even surpassed the healing benefit of her famous German dumplings.

That's why it seemed sadly ironic that, now, friends and family sat at *her* bedside. When Madge learned about her fatal illness, she'd insisted on staying home. "To be surrounded by my angel collection," she beamed.

Madge's colossal collection of angels—1,500 to be exact—had started with just a few Christmas tree ornaments and occasional figurines she picked up at souvenir shops or garage sales. But it didn't take long for her sons to discover that contributions to Madge's plethora of angels were the perfect solution to the what-to-get-Mom dilemma. Soon every friend, neighbor, grandchild, and in-law bought her an angel for every holiday, birthday, and anniversary. It wasn't long before her tiny cottage overflowed with a host of heavenly beings.

She proudly displayed many of them year-round on shelves, the coffee table, end tables, and on top of the TV. In the guest room, she assembled a choir of angels—she reserved that room for musical figurines. Hundreds of singing, twirling, dancing angels crowded antique shelves, hutches, and bedside stands.

Each year on the first day of November, Madge began the month-long process of bringing out the rest of her collection. Angels graced her Christmas tree and the floor beneath it, then cascaded everywhere, from the buffet, to the mantel, to the bathroom sink—to the top of the refrigerator! To Madge, each angel was a reminder of a special person who loved her. She inscribed the name of the giver on the bottom of each angel, along with the date she had received it. She gave explicit directions: "When I pass through the Pearly Gates, make sure every angel goes back to the person who gave it to me."

Now, with a hospice nurse and Madge's two sisters staying with her, that loving task seemed imminent. Her grandson, Troy, stopped by to spend some precious time with his grandma. Sitting on the edge of the bed, he tenderly caressed her hand. "You've been an angel to us all, Grandma—a true gift from God." Troy was the last person to visit his Grandma Madge. A few hours after he left, she entered through those Pearly Gates.

Her sisters, Renee and Gladys, and the hospice nurse gathered in the living room, marveling at how Madge had died with the same dignity, courage, and grace with which she had lived. A faint melody interrupted their discussion. Bewildered, they turned their heads, trying to discover the source of the music. As they crept toward the guest bedroom, the tune grew louder. There, on a table, one lone angel played the song "Cherish" from beginning to end. Then it stopped. With trembling hands, Gladys picked it up and read, "From Troy, 1992." Gladys held the figurine to her chest. "Thanks, Madge, for letting us know you've joined God's heavenly collection of angels."

*Sometimes we hear a soft voice,*
*sending a message of hope and endurance.*
*Remember angels are messengers from*
*a place far beyond our own.*
*We do well when we listen.*

# A Tiger for Baby

T WAS THE ugliest thing they had ever seen. Jennifer and Ron looked at the huge stuffed tiger with the big red bow around its neck and both held back the urge to roll their eyes. But out of politeness for Rhonda, Jennifer's good friend who had given her this baby gift, Jennifer kept her cool and simply said, "Oh, what an unusual gift!" while Ron nodded dumbly in agreement.

"Put it by the baby's crib," Rhonda squealed, delighted with her gift choice. "The baby will love it!"

Jennifer nodded and smiled sweetly, handing the tiger to Ron. They exchanged an "I don't know what to do with it, you deal with it" look between them, and Ron went upstairs to little baby Annie's nursery. Jennifer and Rhonda followed behind him, talking quietly about the baby.

Annie was fast asleep in her crib. She was only three months old, but, thank heaven, she already was regularly napping. Ron placed the tiger near the crib where Annie could see it when she awoke. He secretly hoped Annie would awaken just then, while Rhonda was in the room, and scream in horror at the sight of the tiger. Maybe then Rhonda would get the hint. When Annie did awaken, her eyes went straight for the tiger. She squealed, all right, but not in horror. In fact, Ron could almost swear the little three month old was actually SMILING at it. It was all Rhonda needed.

"She loves it! I told you so! It will be her special guardian," Rhonda gushed, proud of herself.

That night, while Jennifer and Ron put Annie to sleep, they discussed putting the tiger in the basement, but when Ron went to pick it up, Annie became distressed. Her crying ended only when the tiger was put back in its place, beside her crib stand-ing sentinel.

"I swear it's glaring at us," Jennifer whispered. "I'm afraid to touch it."

"I know, it really bugs me the way those eyes watch you no matter where you are in the room. You really think she likes it?" Ron asked.

"Like it? She loves it! Did you see her smiling at it? She never smiles at me, and I feed her!" Jennifer answered.

Each time they tried to take the tiger away, Annie loudly protested. Finally, they gave up and gave in, and Annie drifted off to peaceful slumber facing her beloved tiger.

As the days went on, Jennifer tried to ignore the tiger, despite the fact that she had to move it every time she wanted to get Annie in and out of her crib. The weeks passed, and she became downright fed up with tripping over it at night when she went to get Annie to nurse her. Three months later, the darned tiger was still there, despite numerous attempts to remove it from Annie's room.

One night, however, Jennifer reached the end of her last nerve, screaming out as she tripped over the tiger while placing Annie back in her crib from a nursing break. "Either I go, or it goes," she demanded.

"Look, we're the adults here," Ron stated, "We're the bosses." And with that, they snuck into Annie's room, and picked up the stuffed tiger, took it down to the basement, and placed it inside a plastic bin so it would be well stored for when Annie was older. Satisfied, they went back upstairs and settled in to watch television.

Sometime later that night, long after Jennifer and Ron had gone up to bed, they were both abruptly awakened by a loud thud. As they sat up in bed, they heard Annie begin to wail. They dashed into her room expecting the worst.

Jennifer stopped dead in her tracks, which caused Ron to run smack into her, almost knocking the both of them over. When he saw what had caused Jennifer to stop, he gasped. There on the floor was Annie, sprawled safely over the stuffed tiger, which had somehow found its way back next to her crib. And good thing, too, because their feisty little six month old had figured out a way to climb up and over the crib side, which had been lowered when Annie was put to bed earlier that night but never raised back up.

Jennifer ran to Annie and picked her up, and as she and Ron cooed and comforted their frightened, but perfectly fine baby girl, they both looked from each other to the tiger to each other again, neither daring to ask the question on both of their minds.

Once Annie was soothed back to sleep, Jennifer put her back in her crib, this time remembering to raise the side so Annie couldn't get over it. She and Ron quietly slipped out of the room, both looking back once to see the stuffed tiger standing guard by the crib, watching them with glowing marble eyes.

Outside Annie's room, Ron asked, "Did you bring the tiger back upstairs after we went to bed?"

Jennifer shook her head no. "I was just about to ask you the same thing," she whispered apprehensively.

Ron just shook his head no, then opened Annie's door a crack and peered in. The tiger was still there. He closed the door.

"I've got the creeps," he said.

"Well, regardless of how it got there, at least it was there to break her fall. She could have really been hurt," Jennifer commented. Ron nodded, and the two of them just stood in the hallway outside Annie's room in total silence, each one thinking the same as the other, but neither quite willing to verbalize their suspicions.

The next morning, Rhonda called, and Jennifer told her the eerie story. Rhonda was delighted.

"I told you so," Rhonda giggled. "It's Annie's guardian angel!"

Jennifer didn't know what to say, so she changed the subject. Jennifer and Ron never spoke of that night again, nor did they ever again try to remove the tiger from its permanent post nearby little Annie's crib.

Maybe, just maybe, Rhonda was right.

*Some may see angels as choirs in robes
with gold on their heads and rainbows
in their wings. More likely though, they are like
caring onlookers, watching and
laughing with pure delight.*

*An angel doesn't have to speak
to be heard, be visible to be seen,
or be present to be felt.
Believe in angels,
and they will always be near.*

# A Porcelain Angel

NGELS APPEAR TO us in times of sorrow and grief to help us mend our broken hearts. After hearing my father's story, I am convinced of it.

I have many fond childhood memories and consider myself very lucky to have been raised by two special parents. Mom and Dad were totally devoted to each other; she was the love of his life. They raised their three daughters with warmth and humor, and they gave us a home filled with love and security.

My mother battled emphysema, and during the last two years of her life, she was confined to a respirator. Dad was always there for her, and as she became ill, their roles gradually reversed. He did the shopping, cooking, and cleaning—caring for Mom as she had done for him all the years prior. He never complained and seemed happy for the chance to care for his beloved wife. One night, she died peacefully in her sleep.

My sisters and I tried to comfort Dad as we all mourned together. A few days after Mom died, Dad said to us, "You know, I've never been alone. I went from home to college, into the Navy, then I married your mother. This is the first time I've been on my own." He was 73 years old. He missed her terribly, the love of his life.

The city my folks lived in had a music and crafts festival along the main street every year. My parents had always enjoyed this event—strolling the streets, enjoying the music, viewing the art displays, and delighting in the general air of friendliness and fun. Once again, the festival was scheduled, but Dad wondered if he'd enjoy it alone. He decided he needed to get out and mingle with people to combat his grief and take his mind away from the solitary life he was now experiencing.

The day of the festival, Dad walked up and down the crowded streets, enjoying the sights, sounds, and smells, but as the heat intensified he found himself getting a little weary. He began to look for a sidewalk

café where he could sip some lemonade and catch his breath.

He heard a voice call out to him,
"Excuse me, sir, would you like to sit
down?" He turned to find a pretty
young woman smiling and motioning to a
chair next to hers.

He graciously accepted her offer, and they began
talking about the fair, the weather, and other general
things that strangers chat about.

As Dad and the young lady conversed, she asked
if he was married. He smiled sadly and began remi-
niscing about Mother. His sorrow and sense of loss
were apparent to the young lady, and she listened
attentively. As Dad relayed the story to me later, he
remarked how surprised he was that "a pretty young
woman would let an old codger bend her ear." *Surely,*
he thought, *she would have preferred doing something a
bit more fun!*

After chatting a while, the young lady smiled
and reached into a shopping bag that was sitting by
her feet. She presented my dad with a gift, saying,

"I bought this for myself because I collect angels, but I'd be delighted if you would accept this. I believe it was intended for you." In her hands was a small porcelain angel, sitting and mending a broken heart.

As my dad recounted this story to me a few days later, we both realized that theirs had not been a chance meeting. An angel had entered Dad's world with a gift to heal his broken heart.

Dad passed on not long after that encounter. He had played a round of golf (his "second love") and, as usual, topped it off with an afternoon nap. He passed away in his sleep, and his heart was finally mended as he rejoined my mother, the love of his life.

As for that angel with the broken heart…it's my most valued possession.

# Angie's Plastic Elephant

M Y GRANDMOTHER BELIEVED that all of us, at least once in our lifetime, would encounter an angel in disguise. Mine came in the being of a 19-year-old mentally challenged woman dressed in a hospital housekeeper's uniform. Her name was Angie.

I was 22 when I met Angie. Seemingly healthy other than some swelling and a few pesky sores on my legs, I was hospitalized for tests. It took four months for them to diagnose an inflammation of my blood vessels caused by systemic lupus, which caused severe leg problems. My right leg was amputated, and I was left with nerve damage and deformity of my left leg and foot. Worse yet, as far as my vanity was concerned, I ballooned from a size 9 to a size 22 from massive steroid intake. The steroids also distorted my facial features and body shape. The crowning blow was the loss of my hair from aggressive chemotherapy. I'd stopped looking in the mirror to avoid gawking at the bald, bloated creature who stared back.

Only Angie seemed oblivious to the ravages of my illness. Every other visitor averted their eyes. Even nurses seemed to look anywhere but at me. My boyfriend, Mike, came less and less, finally fading away altogether. In my worst moments, I imagined God turning away also.

But Angie! My angel. The clinking of her massive key ring announced her arrival each morning. I found myself looking forward to her somewhat awkward attempts to mop my floor. The huge industrial mop proved too cumbersome for her jerky, hesitant body movements. But what she lacked in cleaning ability, Angie made up for with her charm.

"Hi," she greeted me daily. She'd walk straight to my bed and look directly at me with her huge brown eyes. "Are you better today?"

She asked with such utter sincerity and hope that I felt obligated to answer "a little better," even on my worst days. Angie would then grin and set about her tasks. While she worked, she shared stories about her mom, her sister, Lucy, and her pet cat, Boo. And sometimes she shared a prayer. Before leaving the room, she never failed to ask if I needed anything.

One morning, during Angie's regular visiting time, I was on a stretcher in the hallway waiting for a ride to the operating room for a bone graft. I'd lost count of the number of such trips I had made in the past few months as surgeons struggled to save my remaining leg. I felt despondent and full of self-pity. God seemed farther away than ever.

A tear trickled down my cheek. As I turned toward the wall to wipe the tear away, I felt a tap on my shoulder. There stood Angie, her face full of love and concern. She pressed something into my hand.

"You hold it," she said. "It always gives me the best luck."

She had placed a blue plastic elephant in my hand; it had always hung on her key ring.

"I won it at the fair," she said. "It's blue, just like your eyes."

I smiled. Through all my ailments and deformities, Angie saw the one part of me that had not changed—my eyes. She loved me the way God did—unconditionally. My spirits soared.

"Thanks, Angie," I said. "I'll take good care of it."

The blue elephant saw me through the surgery, then months of physical therapy and rehabilitation in a different hospital building. The grueling job of learning to live again took most of my time, but I found myself missing Angie. Once in a while, she would stop by my new room on her way home and visit for a few minutes before she had to leave to catch her bus. She always had a funny story about Boo's latest feline escapades. Those were my best days.

When the morning of my discharge finally arrived, Angie was right there. She insisted I keep the elephant. "So you'll remember me," she added.

I gave my friend a big hug. "I'll always remember you, Angie."

She grinned. "You're my special friend. I'll remember you, too."

Over the next few years, I sent notes and cards to Angie through the housekeeping department of the hospital. Then one day my letter was returned. Angie no longer worked there. She had moved with her family and left no forwarding address. But I still have contact with Angie through the little plastic elephant that sits on my mantel.

No other gift will ever compare to this treasured gift of unconditional love from an angel in disguise.

*In the most unlikely of places—*
*waiting in your shadow, perhaps—the most*
*improbable of angels waits for you.*

# Mother's Music Box

*I* WAS HAVING AN especially stressful week. My family, my job, even the other people at church were pushing my nerves to the breaking point. I was getting ready to scream or cry, and I was not sure which it would be.

I was standing in my kitchen having my morning cup of coffee when, suddenly, from out of nowhere, I heard music. I wondered why the ice cream truck was coming so early in the morning. And then I realized the sound was coming from the top of my piano, where my music box collection was displayed. I raced into the living room and was amazed to see my mother's golden angel circling around. The melody "Look for the Silver Lining" rang joyously in my ears.

No train had rumbled by, no jets had passed overhead, no hand had touched the music box.

My mother had passed away ten years before, yet I knew she was still reaching out to me in some miraculous way, encouraging me to have a positive attitude about life.

The mechanism on my mother's angel, now my angel, had worn out ages ago and hadn't played for several years. But that little music box sprang back to life that day—when I needed it most—uplifting my attitude and encouraging me to look for the best in whatever I encounter.

How grateful I am for that revitalizing melody. I have no doubt that my mother's tender spirit sent me those notes of joy.

Since that day, I have tried again and again to get the angel to play its sweet music, but to no avail. I guess if I really need to hear that song again, an angel will intervene.

*Life is full of moments that only you and your angel share.*

*Celestial beings, messengers of light,*
*the neighbor next door,*
*even a passing stranger—*
*angels come to us in many forms.*
*Be open to receive them.*

*Bungling, blundering, feeling so alone,*
*we struggle through some days only to find*
*when the fog has lifted we are just where we should be—*
*in the company of angels.*

# An Afghan from Jan

Standing only two feet tall, it wasn't much of a Christmas tree. They decorated it with a popcorn strand and put a tinfoil star on top. It was all they could afford.

Neil's latest assignment had placed him and his new wife, Jan, in a foreign country with no family or friends. Nevertheless, the delight of their first year together made the spirit of Christmas more special than ever, and they relished the opportunity to reflect on the true meaning of the season.

They sat by their tree on Christmas Eve and took turns reading the story of Jesus' birth from the book Jan's parents had sent them. It was a beautiful book—definitely the most expensive item they owned. When they finished reading, they decided to exchange their gifts.

Neil picked his up first and handed it to Jan. She gently unwrapped it and found a pair of costume earrings inside. "They're beautiful," she said as she clipped them on.

Jan then proudly handed Neil his present. He opened it to reveal a knitted blue cap. Neil grinned. Looking over at Jan's knitting bag in the opposite corner of the room, he inquired, "Did you make this?"

She nodded, smiling proudly.

Neil was touched. The time and thought Jan had put into his gift made it worth much more than the price of its yarn.

"You're wonderful," he whispered, leaning over to give his new wife a loving kiss.

For the next several years, Neil wore the blue cap every winter, even after they could afford nicer ones. They eventually bought a comfortable home and raised three children there. For 25 years, their lives together were blessed. But once the kids were grown,

Jan was stricken with a serious disease. Although she fought this illness for several years, she ultimately lost her battle.

Shortly afterward, the family decided it was time to remove Jan's belongings from the house. Neil wasn't sure he was ready yet, but he reluctantly agreed. He sat on the bed and watched his daughters rummage through the closet, removing all of Jan's clothes.

Watch. That's all he could bring himself to do—and even that was extremely difficult. At one point, his oldest daughter came across the old knitted blue cap. She turned around, holding it toward him, and said, "I remember this. You wore it all the time when I was little."

Neil seized the cap. His eyes reddened, and tears streamed relentlessly down his cheeks. His daughter sat down beside him, put her arm around his back, and rested her head on his shoulder.

"It's OK, Dad," she said. "They're only clothes. We're still keeping Mom in our hearts."

Neil looked down at the floor to hide his grief, but he nodded his acknowledgment.

"Hello...." A voice called from the other room. It was Neil's mom, stopping by to cook dinner. Her mother had come along as well. They all sat down in the living room. Neil looked over at his grandmother and contemplated how lucky he was that she was still around. Not only was she in her nineties, but she was still very witty. He sulkily contemplated how ironic it was that his wife hadn't outlived his grandmother. Jan should still be here, he thought; her life was short-changed and, therefore, so was his.

His grandma interrupted his brooding. "Neil, do you care if I have that knitting bag over there? It's not yours, is it?"

"No, you can have it."

Of course, it wasn't his. The question was just a way to avoid mentioning that it had been Jan's and that she would not need it anymore. Actually, he was surprised that his grandma wanted it. He didn't think her fingers were as operational as her intellect. However, he knew she had knitted frequently in her youth. Maybe she'd get some use from it.

As he reached down to get the bag for her, he noticed several skeins of blue and cream yarn inside with about six inches of knitted rows resting on top. Jan had renewed her knitting hobby after becoming confined indoors. He recalled walking in on her unexpectedly one day and seeing her working with the blue yarn. She quickly put it away as if she was embarrassed. Unfortunately, she didn't finish whatever she had started, and now it would never be completed.

Neil handed the bag to his grandma, who looked happy and eager to take it. Apparently it meant more to her than he thought. Neil wished he could be happy, yet even if he could, he wouldn't. It didn't seem right. How could he feel happiness when Jan was robbed of the same privilege?

Eventually it was time to face his first Christmas without Jan. Being together with the rest of the family was enjoyable, but it also made it extremely obvious that Jan was missing. He looked around at the decorations. His children had bought him a tree after realizing that he wasn't going to. Then they got out the Christmas boxes and put up the familiar adornments. Although he didn't feel like celebrating, he appreciated their attempt to raise his spirits.

Everything was in its usual place just like every other year, but Jan's absence made the celebration awkward. They were doing things differently. Anything Jan had usually done had to be absorbed by someone else. It also took longer to get anything started, similar to the way activities are delayed when waiting for a late guest to arrive. Then the realization would sink in that everyone was already there.

After dinner it was time for presents. Neil wasn't in the mood for gifts, but he could tell that everyone had put more thought into them this year—especially his. Instead of socks and cologne, he received pictures, concert tickets, an original poem, and a book about baseball—his favorite pastime.

Finally, the only gift left to open was the one from his grandma. It was soft and rectangular—probably a sweater. She usually didn't spend much, but she probably wanted to give him something special this year. He began tearing off the paper. His spirits started to rise as he realized what was inside: a magnificent blue and cream afghan.

Neil held it up and asked his grandma in disbelief, "Did you make this?"

She nodded her head, smiling proudly.

"I didn't think you could."

"It wasn't easy. My eyesight's bad, and my hands ache, but that little knitting bag caught my eye for a reason. It contained the beginning of an afghan I knew Jan was making for you. It's as much from her as it is from me, you know."

He did know. Jan began their life together with a knitted gift of love, and near the end of her life she had tried to make another such loving gift for him. Even though she wasn't able to finish it herself, his grandma had somehow gotten the message to get the afghan ready for him by Christmas.

Neil brought the afghan to his face, caressing it. Jan's presence overcame him in a sweep of joy, and he could feel her smiling down on him. She had helped him get through this Christmas, and Neil knew then that her love would be with him forever.

*Angels sometimes come in choirs and sometimes come alone; but they come most often when they aren't expected.*

*Angels do the work of love. Love around us, love within us, love compelling us, and love igniting us.*

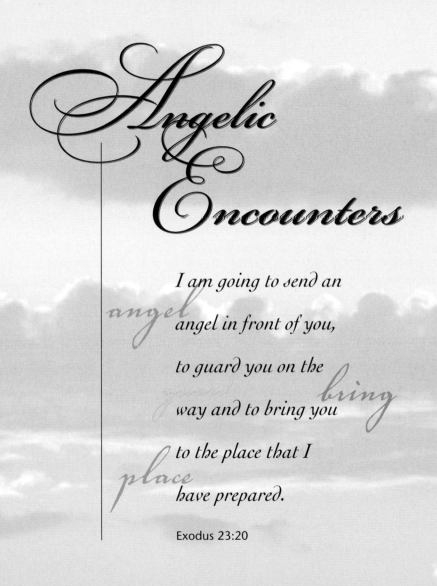

# Angelic Encounters

I am going to send an
angel in front of you,
to guard you on the
way and to bring you
to the place that I
have prepared.

Exodus 23:20

# Encounter With a Street Person

OH, I FELT good about myself. I was so pleased with what a nice, kind, thoughtful person I was. I'd just spent hours laboring away at volunteer tasks, giving my time to help others. I'd helped take care of patients in a nursing home, reading letters to them and chatting with them. My head was full of self-congratulation. I was feeling incredibly virtuous, wonderfully delighted with myself, absolutely superior to lesser folk who were too selfish and preoccupied to reach out to those in need.

Fully absorbed in myself and what a great person I'd become, I scarcely noticed the grubby stranger heading my way. He aimed straight at me as if I were the only person out on the streets that day.

240

When I suddenly noticed him, I braced myself. *Uh, oh!* I could see his filthy clothes, torn and stained. Clearly he'd spent months on the streets, perhaps living in doorways or beneath bridges, huddled in boxes or wrapped in newspapers for warmth.

I dreaded the confrontation. Being approached by homeless people made me feel immensely uncomfortable. I knew I should try to help but felt unable to do anything. If I gave someone cash, it might be used badly. And what else could I do? Besides, I didn't have much money anyway. Finances were tight. Every penny counted. In fact, I was walking home to save bus fare. With the coins I'd saved, I could buy myself a little treat, maybe an ice-cream cone as a reward. I'd earned a treat. I deserved it.

As he neared me, I tensed. It was my money, after all. I worked hard to earn it. I had a right to keep what I'd earned. I had a right to spend it the way I wanted. I shouldn't be expected to give away my hard-earned cash to someone who wasn't working. Braced and tense, I watched as he drew close.

"Can you spare a few cents?" he asked, his hand stretched toward me. I drew back, without actually moving. I thought of the money in my purse. So little of it. And it was mine, all mine.

I opened my mouth to make excuses, to tell him I didn't have any money, to lie and brush him away. His eyes pierced mine as I spoke, and I found myself telling him the truth, or at least part of it.

"I don't have much money. Nothing to spare," I told him. In a way, it was true. Money was tight, and I made sacrifices for every treat, like walking those extra blocks to work and back.

Those eyes pierced through my self-satisfaction, my self-righteousness, my selfishness.

"I understand," he told me, his voice deep and steady. And I thought he did understand. Exactly. I thought he saw right through me, into my greedy spirit. I thought he knew somehow just how much money I carried and what I planned to do with it. He seemed to see into my heart and hear the echo of my childish desires. It was my money. I didn't want to share. Why should I? I wanted it for myself.

Then, still holding my gaze, he said, "I have not always been as you see me now," then he walked away, back straight, dignified in his ragged clothes. He passed behind me, and I stood, stricken and bereft, feeling ashamed of myself.

How could I be so selfish, so greedy, so unkind? Even with so little cash, I could share what I had. I could treat us both to some small treat. We could go together to a nearby snack bar. My money would surely stretch for us both.

In those seconds, I whirled to call him back. He was gone. There was no one behind me. The sidewalk was empty. There were no doorways to slip inside. No cars to duck behind. No alleyways to vanish into. In those moments when I was feeling shame for having been selfish, he'd disappeared.

I never saw him again. But in that moment, staring down an empty sidewalk, I knew. That homeless stranger in his bedraggled clothing had known I was not as good and kind and thoughtful as I liked to think I was. He'd known the hidden selfishness in me. He'd known me.

And suddenly I knew him. He'd given me a clue, hadn't he? He'd warned me that he hadn't always been as I saw him then. And I thought of the Bible quote urging hospitality to strangers, that you might be entertaining angels unaware.

For that was what he was. I'm as sure of it as I am of anything. That homeless, ragged stranger, begging coins of me, had been sent to remind me that I was nowhere near as good as I thought I was. He'd pierced my hard and superior attitude.

I thought about those moments for a long time. I rehearsed what I should have told him, what I wished I'd said. I practiced conversations in case he returned to give me another chance. I searched for his face on my walks from then on. But he didn't return. I guess he'd done what he meant to do. He'd taught me a valuable lesson about myself and others. He'd taught me not to think so highly of myself, not to feel so pleased with me. And he taught me not to judge others too easily.

Behind the next stranger in rags there might lurk an angel in disguise.

*Do not neglect to show hospitality to strangers,*
*for by doing that some have*
*entertained angels without knowing it.*

Hebrews 13:2

# The Waiting Room

R. RAMSEY WANTED to ride with his wife in the ambulance, but the paramedics said he would need his car to get home. He had no choice but to let her go to the hospital without him. By the time he dressed, found his car keys, and locked the house, the sound of the siren had long since faded in the distance.

The drive to the hospital took forever. Every light turned red just as he got to it. Because of the new construction in the emergency room parking lot, he had to park nearly two blocks away, even though it was the middle of the night. Arthritis and old age kept him from quickly covering that distance.

He pushed past the security guard at the hospital entrance and hurried to the check-in desk. "My wife," he said breathlessly, "where is she?"

The receptionist looked confused. John tried again: "They just brought her here by ambulance. They thought she was having a heart attack."

"Oh, you must be Mr. Ramsey." The receptionist smiled. "They've already moved her up to the OR. As soon as we get the paperwork filled out, I'll help you find the surgical waiting room."

Mr. Ramsey tried to concentrate on answers to a long list of questions: "Name?" "Florence Ramsey." "Age?" "Eighty-two." "Your insurance card?" He handed it over. Somehow he managed to give the answers the receptionist needed to complete the form. She then printed out a copy for him to sign. Tears clouded his eyes. His hand shook so much that his signature looked like the wiggly line on a heart monitor.

"Thank you, Mr. Ramsey," said the receptionist. "Now I'll show you the way to the surgical waiting room."

Mr. Ramsey followed her into the main section of the hospital. Their footsteps reverberated in the nearly empty hallway. "Kind of peaceful at night, isn't it?" she asked.

John hadn't the strength to answer. Worry had sapped all his energy. He walked beside her like a frightened child.

"Here we are," she announced. "Someone will find you after your wife's surgery." She pointed out the coffeepot. "Probably not too fresh. The bathroom is right here, so you won't have to worry about missing the doctors."

"In the daytime," she continued, "there's always someone at the desk, and this room is bustling with activity. It seems awfully lonely right now." She pointed to the phone. "Do you have anyone you'd like to call to come wait with you?"

John shook his head. The children lived too far away. He wouldn't worry them till he had definite news. The only person who could have helped him endure the wait was Florence herself. *How strange,* he thought, *that she wasn't there with him when he needed her most!*

"I wish I could stay," said the receptionist.

He wished she could, too. At least her chattering helped fill the silence.

The receptionist patted his shoulder. "I'll be praying for your wife," she said as she slipped away.

Mr. Ramsey also prayed. He squeezed his eyes shut. "Please, God," he whispered. "Don't let her die!"

When he opened his eyes, a young woman was sitting on the couch opposite him. "Are you waiting, too?" he asked.

She nodded, then reached out to shake Mr. Ramsey's hand. "My name's Christina."

"Nice to meet you," said Mr. Ramsey.

"I heard you praying," said Christina. "You must have a loved one who's sick."

"It's my wife," explained Mr. Ramsey. He told Christina about how he had to call 911. "The paramedics restarted her heart and rushed her to this hospital. They are operating now."

Christina had lots of questions. Mr. Ramsey told her about how he and Florence met. "Nearly 62 years ago," he announced proudly. He told her about the fun they'd had together over the years, and he showed pictures of their grandchildren. Each time Christina noticed Mr. Ramsey looking at his watch, she reassured him, "They have wonderful doctors here. Heart surgeries just take a long time."

The first light of dawn was filtering through the window when Christina said, "I have to run upstairs for a bit. I bet you won't have to wait much longer for some news."

Christina was right. Shortly after she left, the doctors arrived, still in their green scrubs and booties. They were smiling. The news was good. Though they had to do a double bypass, the prognosis was excellent. Her chest was closed with staples, but she would be up and around in no time.

Mr. Ramsey shook their hands and thanked them. As they turned to leave, Mr. Ramsey asked, "How is the other surgery going?"

The doctors seemed confused. Mr. Ramsey explained that Christina had been waiting with him through the long, long night. "I guess I was so busy telling her about Florence," he said, "that I just plain forgot to ask which of her family members she was waiting on."

The doctors looked at each other. "Your wife," said one of them, "was the only person operated on at this hospital last night."

*Each angel is special and unique like the human they were given to watch over.*

# A Lift for a GI

WHEN I HEARD the huge metal gates clang shut at the Brooklyn Army Depot that late afternoon, I glanced at the empty parking lot and realized I was alone—and lost. My mind immediately flashed to my wife and two young children, who were waiting for me miles away in New Jersey. My only goal was to get to them as quickly as I possibly could.

I had arrived that morning in April 1959 at McGuire Air Force Base in New Jersey from an overseas tour with the Air Force in France. After clearing customs and immigrations, I checked my wife and two children, ages one and three, into the guest house, then left with four other sergeants for the Brooklyn Army Depot to get our cars that had been shipped from St. Nazaire on the French coast. We had agreed to stay together

and drive back in a convoy with the one who lived in the New York area in the lead; otherwise, we had been told we could get hopelessly lost in the traffic.

An attendant at the Army Depot located my car only to discover the rear bumper had been badly bent in loading or unloading. That meant someone with authority would have to inspect the damage and fill out the proper forms. This was sure to take a while. By the time the damage report was completed, the Depot was closing, and I discovered that my companions had given up on me and left.

Panic gripped me as I listened to the roar of the late afternoon traffic. Since my driving had been limited to country roads and small towns, the very thought of trying to drive through New York City's rush hour traffic overwhelmed me. Even worse, I had no idea how to get back to McGuire Air Force Base, and I remembered the horror stories from GIs who had been lost in New York City. All I could think of was my wife and two precious children waiting anxiously to see me. I was impatient to rush back to the guesthouse, throw my arms around my family, and revel in being together again. After having been apart from them overseas, waiting a few hours seemed like an eternity. What, I asked myself, if I became hopelessly lost trying to find my way back to McGuire? What if I had a bad accident? I was not in the best condition to drive, for I hadn't slept in more than 24 hours. What was I to do? At that moment I could think of no better solution than prayer.

"Lord," I asked out loud, "please help me. I don't know what to do." Then I rested my head on the roof of the car and prayed silently.

After about a minute, I heard, "Hello, Sarge," and looked up to see a young man approaching. "Wouldn't be going to McGuire, would you?" he asked.

I nodded.

"I'd like a ride," he said. "I'll even drive for you if you'd like. This traffic is murder if you're not used to it." Then, as if it was an afterthought, he opened his wallet and presented an ID card. "Air Force, like you," he said.

Although I had been warned about strangers loitering outside military installations, some with stolen or forged ID cards, I felt no fear of this man.

"In my spare time I bring cars from McGuire over here for the guys who are going overseas," he explained. "Then I catch rides back to McGuire with those who've picked up their cars that have been shipped back. Lucky for me you were still here."

I started to say, "Lucky for me you showed up," but I suddenly questioned whether luck had anything to do with it. I had just prayed.... Had the Lord already answered that prayer? "I'll be happy to let you drive," I said. "You're the answer to my prayers."

To this day I don't know why the stranger appeared at that time. Why had he come from the opposite direction instead of from within or around the Depot? Why had he come back when he knew the Depot would be closed? And why had I been so trusting of him, so much at ease as he drove to McGuire?

At no time did I fear he might rob me and take my car. And why did he refuse to let me drop him off at his quarters when we arrived at the base? He just got out at a parking lot and walked away. Was it mere chance that brought him to my aid that afternoon? Or had God anticipated the crisis and delegated an angel on Earth? I don't know for sure.

But when I arrived at the guesthouse at McGuire Air Force base that afternoon and saw my wife and children on the porch waiting for me, I whispered a prayer of thanks to God for bringing me safely back to my loved ones. And I thanked God for the stranger. Whether his appearance was coincidental or an intervention of divine providence, to me he was an answer to my prayer.

*The Lord . . . will send his angel with you and make your way successful.*

Genesis 24:40

# Exit

*I* WAITED FOR THE answering service to connect the caller. Crisis-line volunteers never answer directly. Rarely did we talk to a client more than once or twice, so I was surprised when I recognized the voice on the other end of the line. It was Denise, a young woman I'd spoken to a couple of times in the past. Both times she'd been badly beaten by her husband, and both times I had urged her to go to the women's shelter to avoid further abuse.

"I can't leave him," she'd said. "I have to stay."

When I heard her voice this time, I felt a mixture of relief and concern. At least she was not in a hospital or, worse yet, the morgue. She was probably calling again after yet another beating.

I carried the phone to thc kitchen and poured a cup of coffee as I listened.

"I'm so glad it's you," she said, when I introduced myself. "I really just called because I hoped they could get a message to you. I wanted to tell you about a strange thing that happened."

"Strange" was not how I'd have described her past beatings, and she wasn't whispering as abuse victims often do. Something must have happened.

Denise didn't wait for my response. "Remember, I told you that our office was moving downtown, and that Dan had wanted me to quit when he heard. He was so jealous because I'd be meeting new people."

"Well," she went on, "last Friday I agreed to work late to get the office set up. Everyone else had already left the building when I finished. I hurried to collect my things and head home. I dreaded facing Dan's accusations that I'd just been out playing around with some other man."

Why, I wondered, did abusive spouses always seem obsessed with the idea that their partners were cheating?

"Anyway," Denise continued, "when I went downstairs to go through the main entrance, it was locked...chained shut from the inside. I wasn't worried at first. After all, a big office building like that had to have lots of exits."

While Denise talked, I recorded her information on the crisis call form.

"I checked the door at the end of the nearest hall," she said. "There was a sign that said 'No Exit.' I tried it anyway, but it wouldn't open. I checked several other doors. Each had a 'No Exit' sign. By then I was getting panicked. I could just imagine the punishment Dan would have in store for me for being so late."

I could imagine it, too...and the longer it took for her to get home, the worse the beating would probably be.

Denise went on. "I was nearly frantic by then, running furiously back and forth. I spotted a fire escape and rushed to it. Once more I was met by a 'No Exit' sign. The fine print explained that in case of fire, all the fire doors would automatically open."

Poor Denise. I understood her fear and frustration.

"By then," she said, "I was terrified. I ran back to the front door and began banging on it. 'Get me out of here,' I yelled. I thought maybe somebody outside would hear me, though I don't know what I thought they'd do. Then I realized someone was behind me. I turned quickly around. An elderly man was standing there. I was sobbing by then," Denise said, and I explained that there was no way out.

"'There's always a way out,' he said reassuringly. 'Just follow me.'

"I followed him through the dark hall to a door I'd not noticed before. It was locked just like the others, but my rescuer reached into the pocket of his overalls and pulled out the key. He unlocked the door. I thanked him and hurried to my car. I still hated to think what would happen when I got home. I got my cell phone out of the glove compartment to call Dan, but even as I dialed our number I thought of the man's words: 'There's always a way out.' I remembered you'd said that, too, when you gave me the number for the women's shelter. I still had the number in my purse. Instead of calling Dan, I called the shelter. That's where I am now."

I breathed a sigh of relief. She was safe! "Thank heavens for the night custodian," I said.

Denise laughed. "That's what I thought, too, until the next day when I brought him a thank-you card. I asked the receptionist to give it to him. She looked at me strangely, and then she told me there was no night custodian."

As I hung up from our conversation, I thought about the night custodian. There may be no night custodian, but there most certainly was a night guardian watching over Denise—complete with invisible angel wings!

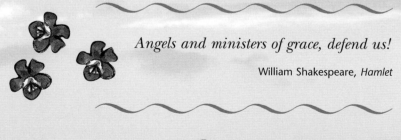

*Angels and ministers of grace, defend us!*

William Shakespeare, *Hamlet*

# A Hug by Accident

I HAD JUST CLEANED out the passenger seat of my police car, tossing an empty water bottle and some old scraps of paper into the trash can. A home-decorating magazine almost went, too, but I hesitated and laid it back on the front seat. I couldn't part with it yet. It had belonged to my mother and was one of many she had shared with me before she became terminally ill and passed away. In a sense, it was like having her with me in the car. I thought of how the last four months without her had dragged on, and the familiar pain of loneliness crept through my soul again. She had been my best friend, an elegant, gracious, and lovely woman. I missed her terribly.

The police radio gave the time, 5:06 P.M., and as I pulled out of the gas station, I was relieved that my shift was almost over. I looked forward to getting home to my husband and two-year-old daughter.

Homeward bound, I drove in the outside lane. It was then I saw a car speeding toward the road I was traveling and run the stop sign without hesitation. The vehicle directly in front of me slammed into the side of the violator's door. In the midst of smoke and fumes, I radioed for an ambulance, almost certain of serious injuries. Citizens stopped to direct traffic as I tried to assist the elderly female victim from her car. She was more confused than hurt, and I gradually coaxed her out of the vehicle and to the sidewalk. I was relieved to see that, other than having a scratch on her face, she appeared unscathed.

As I asked for her name and information, I felt a strange connection to her, even though we'd never met before. She was slender and wore a navy blue dress. She told me her name was Mytrice. I stopped her in mid-sentence and told her, "You're beautiful." I was shocked at my own candor.

"I'm an old woman," she replied. "I'll be 76 on my birthday." She told me she was on her way home from a funeral and my comment had made her feel better. A tear fell to her cheek. I put my arm around her and told her I would call her husband to come to the scene.

A little later, as the wrecker hooked up both vehicles and the "at fault" driver was taken to a local hospital to be checked for back injuries, I bid good-bye to Mytrice and her husband and headed home to my family.

That night I lay still in the darkness, my husband asleep beside me. I thought again of Mytrice and wondered how she was feeling. I couldn't understand why she was still in my thoughts. Usually I just deal with the people and incidents I encounter, then move on with rarely a second thought. But this woman had become embedded in my mind.

The next morning was the same; I kept thinking about Mytrice. I found her address in my notebook and drove to her house.

Mytrice's husband looked quite surprised to see me when he answered

my knock. He invited me to come inside and then called for his wife to come to the living room. As Mytrice rounded the corner, her eyes lit up, and she happily shook my hand. We sat down and chatted, and she thanked me for stopping by to check on her. I couldn't stay long, but I enjoyed our brief visit. I felt at ease and comfortable with her, and she seemed to feel the same about me.

Half an hour flew past, and as I headed to the front door, Mytrice handed me a scrap of paper and asked for my address so she could send me a thank-you note. I told her it really wasn't necessary, but she insisted.

"Can I have a hug?" she asked. She expressed her emotions as freely to me as I did with her, and I was surprised by my response.

"Yes, I could use a hug." I did my best not to cry as she put her arms around me. She held me close and patted my back. What was wrong with me? I had no reason to cry, yet her hug made me feel like a child again. I had to force myself to let go, and as I stood

back, she looked into my eyes and softly spoke.

"I love you. . . . " It was straight from her heart and genuine.

"I love you, too," I managed to whisper as I stood holding her hands. Her eyes spoke to me, and I felt as if I had known her all my life.

"Come back anytime!" she offered as I started down the path of stepping stones that led to my police car.

"I will," I answered and waved good-bye. I was digging the keys from my pocket when I heard the front door open.

"Deputy! Mary has something to give you," her husband shouted.

"Who's Mary?" I asked, puzzled, as I walked back toward the house.

"Oh, it's Mytrice's nickname," he answered as she hurried past him out the door.

"Wait!" she said excitedly. "Please take some of these cookies I baked. You can share these treats with your family."

As I drove away from the red brick house, I felt a jumble of emotions. I had just enjoyed the nicest visit with someone I thought I had met by "accident." Yet, now I wasn't so sure our meeting had been pure coincidence. That sweet someone I'd so recently met shared the same kindness, the same comforting hugs, and the same name with someone very special to me—my own mother, Mary.

*Life seems to run wild,*
*but God holds the reins,*
*and angels tend the harness.*

# Curly Hair

CHRISTMAS WAS ALWAYS a hard time of year for me, and one Christmas Eve, about 40 years ago, was no different. I was 19 years old and about halfway through beauty school. This particular day our schedule was really hectic, and when the supervisor told me about my next customer, I became especially irritated. The lady coming in was in a wheelchair and almost completely crippled. Her caregiver would help me get her hair washed, and then I would be on my own. I knew this customer would take extra time, and I was already feeling swamped.

Once the woman's hair was washed and her caregiver left, we had a chance to talk. She was probably in her 50s at the time, and she told me that the previous year she had lost her husband and her only child, a son. The remaining family members she had left were a couple of cousins.

She hesitated a moment and, with a beautiful smile on her face, said, "But you know, God is so wonderful that he gave me naturally curly hair so I would not have to worry about taking care of it. I am truly blessed." Talk about putting life into perspective.

I am sure that woman has gone to be with God by now, but I still think of her almost every day. No matter what circumstances I face, I still hear her smiling voice saying, "God is so wonderful." She never knew what an impact that simple statement had on me, but I thank God for sending her into my life just when I needed her most.

*Angels are all around us,*
*as far as the heart can see.*

# Stranger on a Hillside

As the steep hillside shimmered before him in the rosy morning sunlight, Reece Hinton yelled and yanked hard on the reins he held in his calloused hands. Maneuvering mules and a wagon down this steep grade was bad enough in good weather, but today, with the roads completely covered in ice, it was next to impossible.

The mules whinnied, their warm breath as white as the snow-covered fields around them. Behind them loomed the wagon full of railroad ties they had been pulling since four o'clock this morning. Hinton, a strong and proud 75 years old, had cut and dressed the ties from his own forest and loaded them into the wagon himself.

Now, however, the old man regretted not bringing along one of his sons or grandsons to help him. If he

tried going down that hill
on his own, he might lose his
wagon, his load, or his mules. At
the least, he risked an accident if the
mules couldn't find footing on the slick
road. At worst, he risked putting himself
and his animals in danger.

But he had gone too many miles to give up now.
Besides, his family needed the money. Bowing his
head and taking a deep breath, Hinton clenched his
hands and hoped for the best. He would need every
ounce of strength possible to keep his wagon from
careening out of control on the way down the steep,
slippery slope. Not enough brake action would invite a
wild plunge. Too much could lock the wheels, jerking
them sideways—and, at the edge of the road, there
was a steep drop-off into a ravine. The mules snorted
and pawed the ground as if they were trying to tell
him something.

Hinton spoke encouragingly to the protesting
animals, then he clicked the reins. As they lunged, he
jerked the wooden brake stick back and forth to main-
tain control.

Inch by inch, they moved forward. Then, though Hinton strived to control it, the wagon began gaining momentum. The mules fought in vain for footing on the slick ice. Hinton struggled with the brake. But between the ice and the downslope and their rapidly increasing speed, he was quickly losing the battle.

Hinton swallowed hard and squeezed his eyes closed, praying for a miracle. He wasn't much of a churchgoer, and he usually left the praying to his wife. But today he began to pray, silently at first, and then out loud as if he were in a prayer meeting. "Help me, Lord!" he cried again and again.

Just then someone called, "Hey, mister, could you use a hand?"

Jerking around, Hinton saw a farmer leaning against the roadside fence. "Sure could," he yelled back, the panic evident in his voice as he fought with the brake stick while tugging on the reins.

In a moment, the stranger reached the wagon. "Can't blame you. This hill is almost impossible when it's iced up like this. Headed into town?"

"Right. Got to deliver this load of ties."

Hinton expected the farmer to help with the reins up front or pull back on the wagon from behind. He did neither. Instead, the stranger just put his hand on the wagon side and walked companionably along-side it in the snow. As soon as he touched the wagon, something remarkable happened. Instantly the mules steadied; the wagon stopped slipping and sliding. They could have been traveling on flat ground! When they finally reached a level stretch of road, the old man reached for his new friend's hand. "You'll never know how much I've appreciated your help." But there was no one there! Now that the danger had passed, the stranger was gone.

Hinton got down off the wagon to look for him, but he found no one. There weren't any footprints in the snow to explain where the man had come from or where he had disappeared to. He couldn't guess who the stranger might have been.

Hinton concluded, "If you need God's help, ask for it. If you're someone he does not hear from very often, be sure to speak up!"

*Guide me, perfect angel,*
*to the place where my spirit can soar*
*free from all earthly limitations.*

*Angels surround our lives with love and protection.*
*Know that they are among us to ease our burdens,*
*shield us from evil, lighten our hearts,*
*and guide us along our journey.*

# Smiles on a Walking Trail

I DIDN'T KNOW HIS name but I recognized his face. Each morning we passed each other on the walking trail around the lake where we exercised. He was a Japanese American, wiry yet spry, in his late sixties or early seventies.

First lap, we'd smile in recognition and say "good morning" as he walked past me going in the opposite direction.

I used this time to reflect and meditate as well as to keep my body toned and flexible. Years ago I used to jog a couple of miles each morning. Then a car accident hurt my back and legs, and even though I recovered, I couldn't jog again. My knees were too weak, so I began walking instead.

Second lap, the man smiled again and held up two fingers as he passed.

I wondered about his life. How does he spend his time when he's not here? What draws him to this place? What milestones has he passed in his life? I pondered the lives of other people on the exercise trail, too, wondering if they were happy or burdened, if they used this time to talk to God as I did.

Third lap, the man laughs gently and holds up three fingers as he passes by again.

I used to get up at 5:15 in the morning and go to the gym with my husband to work out with weights and machines. But time and life had put an end to that. I ruptured a disk in my neck, and after corrective surgery to remove the disk, I began long, torturous hours of physical therapy. I became depressed and discouraged after months with no improvement; my arm was weak, and I was in constant pain. A nerve had been damaged in my right arm and shoulder, so I could barely carry a gallon of milk, let alone lift weights. I had to quit my job as a bookkeeper and office manager, since using a computer for long periods of time caused swelling and pain. I finally had to admit that my life would need some adjustments. Now I was just starting to get into some new routines.

Fourth lap, we were both breathing a little harder, and our steps seemed to be a little slower. But the man smiled as he greeted me again with four fingers lifted in the air.

"One more," he cheered as he walked past.

I was feeling tired and had thought about cutting my walk short and heading home. But I didn't want to let the man down. His optimism and enthusiasm encouraged me to go one more lap with him. I figured if he could go one more lap at his age, surely I could too. I then picked up my sagging rhythm, lifted my head, and walked.

I looked at the scenery around me. The lake, surrounded by trees, was serene. Birds were singing and looking for food, colorful flowers were blooming all around, and the morning sun was shining up above. I smiled and breathed deeply, filling my lungs with crisp, fresh air.

The man waved as we finished our fifth lap.

"See you tomorrow!" he called.

I wondered if he realized how much encouragement he had given me. So often just a smile, a kind word, or a friendly wave is enough to lift my spirits and keep me going. I hope that I can do the same for others who need a little encouraging, too.

"Yes, I'll see you tomorrow!" I called back, already anticipating the next day's walk.

*Listen for your angels,*
*and they'll sing you a tune.*
*But you must listen closely.*

# Stamps for the Hungry

EVERY NIGHT WHEN I pray, I reflect back on the day and thank God for his many blessings. As I do this, I realize just how many times each day the Lord reaches out to touch my life. Although each blessing is important to me, one series of events from December 1991 stands out as being particularly special.

I was getting over a stroke, wearing a brace on my left leg and foot, and still using a walker. I had come a long way, and each day I felt a little better than before, but no one was sure if I'd ever walk unassisted again. My husband was also struggling with his health. He'd been forced to take an early retirement after suffering a stroke a few years before mine. Although his health had improved, his blood pressure remained high. The monthly cost of his medication was really putting a strain on our budget. I applied for food stamps, and we were approved.

When the first envelope came in the mail, it was very thin: It contained only 12-dollars' worth of stamps. I told my husband that so few food stamps would not help us, so I was just going to send them back. I called my caseworker and explained the situation. She said she'd review the case to see if there had been a mistake and would call me back as soon as possible. I put the stamps in my handbag so I wouldn't lose them.

A week or so later, my daughter and I went shopping. On our way home, we turned off the interstate, and at the end of the ramp on our exit we saw a man holding a sign that read, "Hungry. Will work for food." My eyes met his, and I froze as we connected. My daughter kept driving, but I couldn't get the image of that man's eyes out of my head. I told my daughter to turn the car around and go back to the man. She pulled into a  parking lot, and I opened my handbag to see how much money I had. I had only a couple dollars and the food stamps. I thought maybe I could give him the money and the stamps, but I knew I might have to give the stamps back to the government.

I remembered the large bill I had been saving. I hadn't spent it because I knew, with our poor health, we would need it later on. But I felt in my heart that the man on the ramp needed it even more than we did.  My faith in God was strong, and I trusted that if we really needed something, he would provide it for us. My daughter took several one-dollar bills from her handbag and told me to give them to the man, too. I rolled the large bill inside the small ones as my daughter parked the car across from the exit ramp. She asked if I wanted her to deliver the money, and I said I preferred to do it myself. I knew she was concerned about me crossing the ramp with my walker.

I made my way up the ramp and motioned to the stopped cars that I needed to cross. As I approached the man, I touched his arm and he turned to face me. He looked at me, and the pain and suffering I saw in his deep, sad eyes was enough to break my heart. I put the money in his hand. He did not look to see what I had given him, and as I turned to walk away he said, "Ma'am, God bless you." I stopped and said, "Thank

you, and may God bless you, too." I looked into his eyes again, and they were bright as diamonds, pretty and light blue. I started back across the ramp, prepared to motion for the cars to let me cross, but I did not have to stop them. Drivers were getting out of their cars to hand money and food to the man. I smiled joyfully as I walked back to the car.

A few days passed, and my son and daughter came to visit me. The TV was on, and there was a story on the news about people with signs that read, "Will work for food." They said it was a sham and encouraged people not to fall for it. My daughter told my son what we had done, and he started to laugh. He said that man probably used the money for drugs or alcohol. But I remembered those stirrings in my heart and trusted that they were from God. I still felt good about what I had done. I said, "Maybe some of the people with those signs really are asking for help to buy food and not drugs or alcohol. I know what I saw in that man was real."

A couple weeks passed, and I forgot about the man on the ramp. Then one day, we received a thick envelope in the mail from our caseworker. I opened it, and discovered that it was filled with books of food stamps! I told my husband we must have gotten someone else's stamps by mistake. He looked over the enclosed letter: The caseworker said there had been a mistake the month before, so we were receiving last month's stamps along with this month's.

We received over $400 in food stamps. As I finished reading the letter, I remembered the most beautiful bright blue eyes, looking like diamonds. I remembered the man on the ramp and knew in my heart he was an angel. No one can convince me differently.

It was shortly after this that I was finally able to take off my leg brace and give away my walker. The blessings of the Lord never cease to amaze me!

# The Visit

JUNE DAYS WERE hot and humid, but those were the days I enjoyed most as a child. Every summer my parents would let me go spend a week with my aunt and uncle, who lived about a hundred miles away. When I was a little girl, it felt like going to another country.

The summer I was ten seemed no different than any other year. I was excited, as usual, to go visit Tom and Rhoda. My dad, however, wasn't sure if I should go. My uncle had recently lost his job, and they were watching every penny. I promised not to eat too much and to help out with the chores. Uncle Tom told my dad to send "that little ray of sunshine" on down, saying they'd miss me too much if I didn't come. So I packed my bags, and off I went.

My aunt and uncle had just bought an old house to fix up, before Tom lost his job. It needed a lot of work, and they'd been counting on Tom's regular paychecks to cover all the repairs. I felt bad for my uncle because now he was forced to do most of the repairs himself. Although he was a smart man, there were some things he just didn't know how to do. Tom never grumbled, though—he was always happy and smiling, saying God would take care of things. I adored him and believed every word he said.

I loved doing work around the old place, and there was plenty of work to do. I was good at yard work, and I also loved using a hammer—my uncle even bought me one of my own. There was also a lot of electrical work to be done. The plumbing was bad, too, and much of the piping needed to be replaced. The roof, however, was my uncle's main priority. He said it wouldn't be much fun if we were sleeping and water started dripping from the ceiling.

The wiring was the other major concern for Tom. He told us at the supper table that, after the roof, it was the most important thing in need of repairs. "If I don't get the wiring done, I'm afraid we might have a fire," he said. I was so scared, I prayed that night when I went to bed that everything would be OK.

The next morning we started working on the roof, trying to make the repairs as quickly as we could. We stopped for lunch, then returned to work. My uncle and I had a great time; he kept me entertained for hours with all his stories and jokes.

In the mid-afternoon, Aunt Rhoda came out and yelled that someone was there to see Tom. We climbed down off the roof and went into the house. There we saw a weathered old man sitting at the table with a beat-up suitcase at his feet. His eyes sparkled, in sharp contrast to all the weary wrinkles on his face. My uncle shook the old man's hand and asked what he wanted.

"I'll be glad to work for a meal," he replied. "I haven't eaten in two days, and I'm very hungry." *What can he do?* I thought. *He looks too*

*old and frail to be of any real help.* Tom asked Rhoda to fix the man some food. "You don't have to work, sir, but you're welcome to stay in our home as long as you need to."

"Anything you want done," the stranger insisted, "I can do." Uncle Tom nodded and helped my aunt serve him lunch.

Tom and I went back outside and returned to work on the roof. Soon the old man came out and asked what he could do. "Just relax under the shade tree today," Tom told him. "Maybe tomorrow you can do some work." We went back to repairing the roof and soon forgot about the visitor. When I remembered him, I looked for him under the tree. Much to my surprise, he was gone. Tom just shrugged his shoulders. "He was probably just a drifter who needed some food. It happens all the time."

I was disappointed. I couldn't forget the sparkle in the man's eyes, and I'd been looking forward to seeing it again. I remembered what my dad used to tell me: "Never turn away a stranger because you might be turning away an angel." As a result, I always

thought I could tell if someone was an angel by looking into their eyes.

When the sun started to go down, Uncle Tom
said it was time to stop working for the day. We
climbed down, put away our tools, and went into the
house. We were both startled to find the stranger sitting in the same chair he'd sat in earlier, his suitcase sitting by his feet. Tom talked to him
for a while, and then we all sat down to
dinner. Everyone was quiet.

Aunt Rhoda spoke first. "We sure do appreciate
you fixing the electricity," she told the old man. My
uncle nearly choked on his food.

"I fixed the fuse box," the man explained. "Seems
you had some bad wiring there. That was the cause for
the fluttering lights when you pulled on the light
strings."

Tom didn't seem to know what to say. The old
man just kept his head lowered and said, "Wasn't too
bad, but needed fixing."

"Thank you so much," said Tom, still obviously
surprised. "That really needed to be done."

The old man didn't say much throughout the evening. He seemed content to just rest and listen to our conversation.

It was late when we all went to bed. Uncle Tom told the stranger he could sleep on the floor in the living room and said he was sorry he didn't have a decent bed for him. The old man nodded an OK, and we all went to bed.

The next day, to our amazement, the stranger helped my uncle fix the water pipes. Tom said he was surprised at how much the old man knew about plumbing. Everyone was thrilled at how much work had gotten done in just two days—and it hadn't cost Tom and Rhoda a thing.

Near the end of the day, the stranger said, "My work here is done. After supper will you take me down the road and drop me off?" Tom asked him to stay as long as he wanted to, but the man said he was needed down the road.

We all had a great time at dinner, although the old man didn't say too much. He looked up once and smiled at me, and I could see a sparkle in his eyes. I couldn't help but smile back.

After supper we all piled into Uncle Tom's truck and started down the road. Since Tom and Rhoda's house was out in the country, we had to drive several miles before we turned out onto the state highway. We had driven about 15 miles when the stranger said, "This is it. I'll get out here."

"But, sir, there's nothing here," Tom replied. "Let us take you to the nearest town." The old man insisted this was where he wanted to get out. Tom stopped the truck. "Sir," he asked, "are you sure you won't let me drive you into town?" The stranger continued to insist this was the place. We all told the man how grateful we were for his help and asked him to stop by if he was ever in the area again. My uncle turned the truck around, and we started back home.

Suddenly Tom stopped and turned back around. "I think we should make sure he gets to town safely," he explained.

We drove back to where we had dropped the man off just a couple minutes before and were surprised not to see him. We kept driving, looking back and forth, up and down the road, but still saw no sign of him. It seemed as though the stranger had simply disappeared.

I believe that stranger with the suitcase was an angel sent to my aunt and uncle in their time of need. And I think he came specifically during my visit, so I'd get to witness him, too. Since then, I've seen that stranger again. He wasn't the same old man I saw as a child, but I know it was him because he had the same suitcase and the same sparkle in his eye. I believe that suitcase contains the names of people who need help and whatever it takes for the angel to help them. And what about the sparkle in his eyes? I imagine that's God's love shining through.

*An angel's song on a lonely night is like*
*a sweet friend's voice.*

# Angelic Creatures

For he will command
*command*
his angels concerning
*angels*

you to guard you in
*guard*

all your ways.

Psalm 91:11

# Stormy's Tree

THE SPRING DAY is soft and warm, brimming with life. I know I should be filled with the giddy sense of renewal that late April has always brought me before. Why then are cold tears running down my cheeks? Why are my fingers trembling so hard that I can scarcely hold my coffee cup while I stare out the kitchen window to the pasture beyond? Because the grass is beginning to green under Stormy's tree.

In all the 30 years he lived with us, the sorrel-and-white spotted pony would never have allowed grass to grow under the sprawling oak at the top of the hill. I can see him now, pawing intently at the soft earth until it met his satisfaction. It was his favorite spot to stand to avoid the hot summer sun, and he chose to be there during even the worst of the winter storms, ignoring the open barn.

My hands begin to steady as I lose myself in memories, remembering when Stormy came to live with us.

"He was in with a load of calves," my husband, Carl, said, after arriving home from the barn sale. He led the shaggy pony out of the trailer. "No one wanted him."

We eyed each other suspiciously, Stormy and I. I knew nothing about ponies, and I could tell he knew nothing about mothers. Randy and Michelle dashed out the front door and mauled the new arrival like young bear cubs. The pony's ears flickered and his eyes widened, but he accepted them calmly. Obviously, he knew a lot about kids.

"Let's name him Lightning," Randy shouted.

"No, I want to name him Thunder," Michelle cried insistently.

Carl grinned and winked at me. "I guess we'll just have to compromise," he told them. "Let's name him, uh, Stormy."

Over the years, I spent countless hours leading Stormy around the yard while giving endless rides to my children. As the years passed, they rode alone and used him for transportation—to the barn, to the pasture, and to the neighbor's. They dropped the reins on the ground and left him until they returned, if they remembered. If they didn't, he'd come home by himself. I'd find him in the back-yard, peacefully munching grass, his reins dragging behind him.

Often, I sat on the back steps, and we shared an apple while I told him my troubles. Somewhere, behind those intelligent brown eyes, I knew he under-stood every word I said. He respected Carl, he loved the kids, but he and I were pals.

We raised the kids together, Stormy and I, and I was never sure who was doing the best job. He was more patient than I could ever be, never once object-ing to whatever they did. He hauled them around with loving care until they grew so tall their feet barely cleared the ground. It wasn't long after that before the pony was retired to the pasture and the big oak.

Stormy was a member of our family, a part of us, and I thought he'd always be there. Until one cold January day when I looked out the window and saw him sleeping peacefully under the oak. The winter wind ruffled his shaggy coat and gently swayed the leafless branches hanging over him, and I knew that he would not be at the gate to greet me anymore.

The memory is too fresh in my mind. I turn away from the window, spilling cold coffee on the counter-top. I don't care. I brush my hair back, angry that it's streaked with gray, knowing it will be grayer tomorrow. I'm furious with my body for growing old, with my kids for growing up, and with Stormy for dying.

"It isn't fair," I cry silently to God, but God doesn't seem to answer me.

The trembling is back while I try to pour another cup of coffee. When I take a sip, I taste salty tears running into the corners of my mouth. My spirits lift when I hear the old truck pull into the drive. Carl has just returned from the Monday trip to the barn sale, but he doesn't

297

come into the house, and curiosity takes me outside. The sheepish smile on his face makes me suspicious.

"She was in with a load of cattle," he tells me. "I couldn't resist."

"She" is a palomino pony, smaller than Stormy, more refined and ladylike. Her ears pitch forward while I approach and my heart turns over. Carl hands me the lead rope and hurries into the house to phone our daughter and grandchildren.

We stare at each other for a long moment, this stranger and I. Finally, I lead her to the gate and turn her loose. She races across the pasture, head up, tail held like a flag. One complete circle of the fences and she slides to a stop under the oak. I hear her funny whiffing noises while she lowers her head and checks out the soft, damp earth.

In a few minutes, my daughter's car pulls into the driveway, and two blonde whirlwinds fly out and scramble across the pasture, screaming with delight. The pony's eyes are wide, but she accepts them without a fuss. She looks at me with an expression that clearly asks, "Am I doing this right?"

"What's her name?" my granddaughters shout. "What's her name?"

I hesitate. Am I ready to put aside the years that have gone by? My heart aches with the pain of knowing I can never go back, but who can say that the years ahead won't be the best? I can't accept this golden pony as a replacement for the little spotted pony who's gone from my life, but perhaps this is my answer from God. Is she a symbol of the wonderful years to come?

I take a deep breath. "Sunshine," I tell them. Then I shout out loud. "Her name is Sunshine!"

I breathe in the marvelous newness of the spring day, my heart singing. Sunshine settles down to the serious business of digging all the grass away from under the oak tree.

# Max the Grinch

WE CALLED OUR dog "Max the Grinch" because, like the Dr. Seuss character, he loved to steal things, especially presents from beneath the Christmas tree. When he was a puppy dragging off shoes, toys, throw rugs, books—anything he could get his mouth around—we laughed. The joke wore thin as he grew into a 75-pound hound who was known to have knocked over a large barbecue grill to snatch the steaks and to have intercepted baseballs in the middle of games.

"What are we going to do about that dog?" The exasperated question came more and more often—until one icy winter day when we found out that he was our very own guardian angel.

After a night of freezing rain, we awakened to a landscape encased in crystal. We kids couldn't wait to get outside. Neither, of course, could Max. With all the gleeful cracking icicles falling from the porch railing and landing on the mirror-bright driveway, no one heard the first telltale crack—except Kathy. Just seven years old, Kathy was happily swinging on a rope suspended from a limb of a big old apple tree near the back steps of the house. At the sound, she looked around momentarily, shrugged, and went back to swinging. Max had been taking full advantage of the commotion, stealing birdseed from a feeder in the neighbor's backyard. When he heard the sound, he looked up and began barking.

"Quiet, Max!" Mother opened the backdoor and called. Max kept barking. With the next crack—a giant pop, almost as if something had exploded—we all turned around to look. The entire apple tree, including the limb upon which Kathy was swinging, was splitting. It seemed to be happening in slow motion. The tree was crashing down toward Kathy as Kathy was staring up at it. Still at the backdoor, my mother screamed; the rest of us yelled, but no one was able to move a muscle. No one except Max, that is.

The big dog bounded across the yard and grabbed the bottom of Kathy's parka in his jaws. He dragged her, protesting, out of the way—just as the first branches crashed to the ground. In fact, he dragged her clear around to the front yard, leaving us all staring at the huge downed tree.

We ran to the front. Covered with snow, angry tears streaking her red face, Kathy was screaming at the oblivious Max. "What did you do that for, Max?" she sputtered.

Mother hugged her, and we hugged Max—until he pulled away to run back for more birdseed. Even an angel has to eat!

*Angels find us not only when we need them most but also when we simply need them.*

# Smokey

H E CAME TO us when we weren't expecting him, but isn't that always the case with angels? A little ball of fur who'd wrap his tiny paws around my neck and stay until I pried him loose. He'd been abandoned on a farm—left on a doorstep with his brothers and sisters. They had named him "Dinky" because he was the runt of the litter. All his feline siblings had gone off to good homes, but Dinky was left behind because he would hide when people came over. We had to drive out to the farm three times before they could find Dinky and bring him to us.

I didn't want a cat. I've never even really liked cats. Too independent. Too difficult to understand. Too demanding and yet aloof. I've always considered myself a tried-and-true "dog person."

It was my daughter who insisted with those big brown eyes and that sweet, pouty lip, and so I'd said we'd go and meet this kitten. No promises. As a single mom working full-time, struggling to make ends meet and already the mother of a bunny rabbit who had somehow insinuated her way into our life, I didn't really think I could handle one more mouth to feed and litter box to clean.

Then Dinky appeared. He gave me that hug and looked at me with those big, scared, "love me" eyes, and I was hooked. I didn't even hear the pleading coming from my daughter. It was already a done deal.

The first thing we did was change his name. We decided "Dinky" isn't a name that any respectable cat wants to grow up with. We surmised that the only reason he was small was because he was too scared to eat. So "Smokey," the little scared orphan, joined our family. It was like having a toddler again. Everything had to be put away; we couldn't leave anything out on the floor, the table, or the counters. And I didn't sleep—every little meow woke me up night after night. I wondered if we had made a mistake in adopting this little misfit.

Then strange things began to happen to me. My normal routine included constantly racing around the house—doing six things at once. I'd throw in a load of wash, run to the computer to work for awhile, and then start dinner while making any necessary phone calls. But that kitty kept getting underfoot. Countless times I accidentally kicked him. He'd run away as if I was going to hurt him. I'd run after him and reassure him that it was only an accident. I was terrified I'd step on him. So without realizing what was happening, I began to slow down.

When I'd go out for a little while, he'd be waiting by the door for me. I tried to rush in and get busy, but he would lie down and meow, expecting that I was

going to greet him, pet him, and love him. I tried to resist. I didn't need a cat running my life. After all, I had things to do. And how could I possibly do it all with these unnecessary stops for petting and playing, feeding and cleaning?

But I couldn't resist that little furry paw reaching out to touch my arm and those big green eyes looking at me in wonder and confusion. That foreign creature tugged at my heart and changed my life. I began to call him to come up onto my lap, and I would sit and pet him. I wasn't on the phone; I wasn't working; I wasn't doing anything at all except petting him.

At first, my mind would race through all the things I should be doing instead of doing nothing. But the thing was, I wasn't doing nothing—I *was* doing something. Without realizing it, I was slowing down. I remembered that it's OK to sit down during the day. It's OK to take a deep breath and run my hand along that furry spine. That little furry angel was teaching me to slow down and remember to enjoy each day and each moment. The runt of the litter seemed to me to be heaven sent to rekindle my love for life—to give a new spark of joy to each day. He didn't care if there were bills to be paid or errands to run. All he cared about was rubbing his head against my leg and reminding me to slow down and pet him—to slow down and enjoy the day.

He's a part of our lives now—a full-fledged family member who commands much respect and attention. And every time I look into those eyes or feel the touch of his paw on my arm, I take a deep breath and thank heaven for sending us a little angel to love.

*A man does not always choose what his guardian angel intends.*

Saint Thomas Aquinas

# A Winged Angel

WALKING THROUGH THE drugstore, I noticed the young salesclerk. Her name tag read "Darla," and I recognized her as the little girl I used to babysit many years before. I watched as she wrote a note to a customer. Darla had been born deaf, and this simple method (despite hours of signing and speaking training) seemed to be her preferred method of communicating with the public.

It must have been more than 20 years since "the event" had taken place. I thought of what could have been, of the tragedy that would have touched so many lives if things had turned out just slightly different.

At the hopeful and young age of about-to-turn 14, I had a thriving babysitting business. I was watching Darla and Billy during the summer months while their parents went to work. Darla had just had a birthday, and she'd gotten her first bike, a metallic blue number with high handlebars and a banana seat. Darla thought she was the coolest thing on two wheels (or four, to be precise, since she still needed training wheels), and I loved watching the joy on her pretty face as she rode her new gift.

Darla's father had insisted that she ride the bike only in the driveway unless he was with her. As he signed this to her, she moaned and turned away—the typical response when she didn't want to "see" what you were saying to her.

"I'll watch her," I promised. "I won't let her out in the street."

He looked worried, but he nodded his approval and left for work.

Darla's brother, Billy, who was jealous of all the attention his sister was getting, was in the yard doing somersaults and cartwheels, desperately trying to draw me to him. Darla rode her bike in the large driveway, circling proudly, waving each time she passed.

Then I heard the squealing tires of a car speeding into the subdivision. They say that a plane crash occurs when more than one improbable calamity occurs at the same time. In a similar vein, our small world seemed about to crash.

First, Billy fell doing a cartwheel and hit his head on a brick. He started crying, and a small stream of blood that ran down the side of his face sent him into hysterics. Darla, unable to hear the sounds of her brother crying or the car speeding in our direction, decided at that moment to try out her new bike in the street. Too late to stop her, I could only watch, my heart pounding so hard it hurt, as she sped out of the driveway. The car was coming closer and closer, and I was powerless to do anything.

Picking up Billy, I ran after Darla, but I did not stand a chance—she had too much of a lead on me. As soon as I saw the car, its driver also saw Darla, who was now in the middle of the street, pedaling and looking up at a small flock of starlings flying overhead. The driver honked and yelled at her, but he did not slow down. In an instant Darla was going to be hit.

"She's deaf! Stop!" I screamed at the car, but his music was up so high that the driver couldn't hear me.

I screamed at Darla to stop, and then I shielded Billy's eyes from what I knew was going to be a horrible scene.

The car flew past me. The driver finally realized that Darla was not going to move in time, so he tried to stop. His brakes screeched, and his front end started to turn as he began sliding sideways down the pavement. The tires smoked, but he couldn't stop the heavy vehicle at that speed.

At just the right moment, one bird from the flock of starlings swooped down in front of Darla and landed in a tree to the side of the road. Darla followed its flight and turned her bike, pedaling to the tree for a closer look. The car, now almost fully sideways, slid behind her, barely missing the back of her bike. Darla stared happily at the bird, never seeing the car that had almost taken her life. The driver swore at her and sped away. But at least she was safe.

That moment, at the impressionable age of almost 14, I began to believe in God and angels and spirits and everything else that rescues small children from certain death. For years I thought about that tiny bird and why it flew to the tree at that exact moment, leaving its fellow travelers to fly on. It confirmed that even the smallest of things can change your life.

A tear ran down my cheek as I stood in the bright, orderly drugstore, thinking about all the tiny, yet profound crossroads in our lives—many of which we're not even aware of. How thankful I was that God sent an angel in the form of a starling to save that little girl's life. I could only imagine what other miracles I'd never even noticed! Surely he puts us where we need to be exactly when we need to be there. Darla finished helping another customer, and I walked over to say hello.

*The days, the hours, the minutes of our lives*
*are guarded and observed by angels.*

*Light as a feather and quieter than snow,*
*your angel flurries through your life,*
*engaged in all your concerns.*

# Angel

M Y HUSBAND, JIM, and I have always been blessed with a house full of cats. We've shared our home with 11 feline friends, all of whom were strays or from an animal shelter. And we always run an "outdoor café" on our porch to feed countless other strays. Weenie, our oldest and dearest cat, died in the fall of 1996, an especially painful time for us because I had recently suffered the loss of my entire family. Over a period of 11 months, my mother, father, and brother had all died of cancer. I was becoming increasingly depressed and could not bear the thought of the normally joyous holiday season without my family and Weenie.

My downward slide became apparent at work, especially to a dear young man named Patrick. He and I had formed a close bond immediately after I started my job. His great sense of humor and love for laughter and practical jokes had instantly drawn me to him—he reminded me a great deal of my brother. I was also one of the few people who could see through the comedian on the outside to find the hurting teenager on the inside, crying out for attention and understanding. We were both from broken homes and had an overwhelming need to be loved. Perhaps that is what had really drawn me to him—in many way, I understood his pain. It disturbed him to see me so depressed, especially at Christmastime. Knowing of my great affection for cats, and how much the recent loss of Weenie had added to my depression, Patrick decided to take action.

He had heard about a poor little kitten that had been left to die, but miraculously, someone had heard her faint cries and rescued her. She was taken to a local veterinary clinic, where she was first fed through an eyedropper and then eventually raised on a baby bottle. She spent the first three months of her life in the clinic, receiving constant love and attention from the staff. Patrick chose the perfect "mama" for this special kitten.

On December 23, he called me into the kitchen at work and gave me a handsomely wrapped package. Immediately being suspicious of a prank, I shook it. The familiar sound of a box of cat food rattled through the kitchen. Everyone who had gathered started laughing, so I went along with Patrick's joke. I ripped off the paper and was holding a box of Kitten Chow. By this time, I was laughing, too, and thanked him. "Well, at least it's something I can always use!" At that moment, he took me by the hand and led me around the corner. There stood another coworker holding the most adorable little kitten I had ever seen! I was so shocked and surprised. I couldn't believe how kind and thoughtful my young friend had been. There aren't many people who would go to such lengths to give such a meaningful gift.

Patrick looked at me and said, "I figured this was the one thing you needed to cheer you up and help you make it through this Christmas. Having a new kitten to care for will occupy your mind and bring you the happiness you deserve!" I was laughing and crying and hugging him at the same time. For once in my life, I was speechless!

As I walked closer to the kitten, our eyes met. There was an instant attraction, and I knew in my heart she was meant for me. She scrambled into my arms, and crawled up the front of my Christmas Cat sweatshirt until her little head was resting on my right shoulder. It was there that she stayed for the rest of the afternoon, purring contentedly. Others tried to take her from me, but she held on to me for dear life. She had adopted me. I named her Angel, and everyone agreed it was the perfect name for this tiny gift from God—and, of course, Patrick.

I took Angel home and introduced her to her new brothers and sisters and my stunned but pleased husband. There was no period of adjustment as there had been with the other cats. Angel walked around as though she owned the place. It seemed so familiar to her, as if she had been here before. It was then that I realized that God had shown her the way, and she had accepted her assignment.

Her first night at home, she wasn't satisfied to sleep in

the cozy little bed we had carefully prepared for her downstairs. Instead, she followed me up the steps and took her place on my pillow. And she did the same thing every night afterward. She placed her paws around my head as if holding me safely and protecting me from the world. I began to sleep more soundly and peacefully than I had in a very long time.

As Angel grew, we needed to change the sleeping arrangements because I no longer had a place on my pillow for me. Now she sleeps right next to me, lengthwise with her head on the pillow nestled close to mine. This gives her close access to my face when she feels the need for hugs and kisses during the night. If I make the "mistake" of trying to roll over and face away from her, she is forced to get up and properly throw herself down again on the other side, letting me know of her displeasure at being disturbed.

Angel always seems to sense when I am having an especially bad day because she makes it a point to stay as close as possible to me and smother me with extra kisses. She and our God always give me the strength and courage I need to go on another day.

Patrick is always anxious to hear of her latest escapades and devilish behavior. She makes us both laugh, even more than we did before, and that is quite an accomplishment.

Because of God's love for me and the special friendship I have with Patrick, as well as the unconditional love and understanding from my husband, I have been able to recover from my tremendous losses and once again I am able to enjoy life. I firmly believe that God sent me the best gift of all that Christmas, and he used Patrick as the deliveryperson.

*I've heard it said that angels live*
*where love and joy begin,*
*Which must mean all my heartbeats*
*are tiny wings within.*

# An Angel with Four Paws

HE NIGHT HAD turned cold when Martha finally ended her shift at the restaurant. She stepped outside to head home. It had been a very busy night, with truckers coming in nonstop from the highway throughout the night, and Martha had worked two hours of overtime to make sure everyone got what they needed. As dog-tired and aching as her feet were, she could certainly use the extra money.

She crossed the street and headed toward the tiny parking lot where she usually parked her car, but the lot was full of trucks and she couldn't spot her small Honda anywhere. Martha stood there for a moment, certain that the hectic shift had gotten to her brain, wondering where on earth she had parked her car. Then she remembered the lot had been full when she

got there. She had parked at Lew's Deli, on the street behind the diner. She ran across the street, scolding herself for being so forgetful. She was working way too hard these days; sometimes her brain just couldn't keep up with all she had to remember.

She headed down the alley to the next street south, certain her vehicle would be right in front of Lew's, which was now closed. It wasn't there. Martha felt a tiny ball of panic begin to bounce in the pit of her stomach. She took a deep breath, not wanting the panic to get any bigger. Her car had to be here some- where, unless, and she hated even giving the thought credence, it had been stolen. Just then she heard a rustling behind her. Turning, she saw a dark shadow in the alley. Panic bore down on her like a freight train as she realized she was within attack distance of a huge, ominous-looking black dog.

The beast had to be almost as big as her, and she wasn't short. Or maybe it was just the eerie way the street lamp cast a glow on the animal, which appeared to be some kind of mutt, albeit a big and threatening one. The dog moved a step toward Martha, its fierce yellow eyes trained on her. Martha felt her throat catch as she tried to scream, to cry out for help. Nothing came out but a soft whimper. She forced her feet to move and took a wobbly step backward. The dog responded, taking another step forward, and Martha realized that she had only two choices: Stay and be attacked, or run and be attacked.

Choosing the latter, Martha held her breath and ran from the dog. She rushed down another alley leading back to the diner. She didn't dare look back, but she heard the thud of the dog's heavy paws following her. She dodged between cars and trucks in the side lot, trying desperately to find her car, and she slammed right up against the cab of a pickup. It took the wind out of her for a second, long enough for her to see the dog coming out of the shadows toward her. She turned, frozen with fear, to face the dog, certain she was about to be attacked. She tried again to scream, to get a word  out of her tight throat, but she could barely croak a whisper. "Why won't you leave me alone?" she hissed at the dog, but the animal stared at her with golden slits of eyes.

Voices off to the side of the lot caught Martha's attention. Gasping for strength, she forced her body in motion, figuring if the dog attacked her now, at least she would have some help. As she followed the voices, she found her own voice again and was about to scream for help when she noticed the source of the voices. She had found her car, parked where she left it in a small alley next to the diner. But she also found two large and very hostile-looking young men in her car, trying to hot-wire it.

As she turned to run before they could see or hear her, the two men looked up. Sensing the threat, they got out of the car and came menacingly toward her. One of them brandished a long knife, and Martha froze as the other man put his hand in his pocket and motioned as if he had a gun. She was about to concede her Honda to them, beg them to take it if they would just let her go when she heard a fierce growl behind her. In a flash of dark fury, the dog that had been following her lunged past her, landing squarely on the two men, knocking them over and attacking them. Martha screamed full force over and over again. Within a minute, several truckers who had just left the diner came to her rescue.

The truckers pinned down the two bloodied and defeated car thieves as Martha ran to the diner to call the police, stopping only to look back at the wonderful dog that had clearly been following her to protect her. But the dog was nowhere in sight.

Ten minutes later the police arrived, questioning Martha and the truckers. Martha told them about the dog, and when the officer did a quick check of the two suspects, the bite marks were evident. The dog had vanished, and now the suspects would have to deal with the possibility of rabies.

But Martha knew, as she got into her Honda to head home, that her guardian angel was not rabid. As she pulled out onto the

main road, something made her glance over to the alley opposite of where the police were finishing their work. There, in the shadows, she could see two bright yellow eyes staring at her. Martha stopped her car, rolled down her window, and whispered, "Thank you." As she drove away, she knew she would see that angelic dog again, perhaps on another cold night when she had worked an extra-long shift and her feet were tired and aching.

*Through strife or storm or darkest night,*
*My angel is there to show me God's light.*

# Beloved Angels

They saw that his
face was like the face
of an angel.

Acts 6:15

# Dear Uncle Edmund

"MY DAD WANTS you to tell your dad that he'll drive Friday night. Why take two cars when we're going to the same place?" The words uttered by one of my classmates reach my ears despite the noisy chatter of three dozen other 13-year-old freshmen rushing through the school hallway to their next class.

"Is your dad's car big enough for the four of us? I don't want my dress to get squished. We should..."

The second girl's voice trails off, and I know it's because my two schoolmates have noticed me standing by my locker. Their topic of discussion is the upcoming father-daughter school dance, but I won't be attending. A father is necessary, and cancer claimed mine just a few months ago.

I pretend to be interested in my locker contents, thus giving the duo a chance to pass me by without comment. In this small, all-girl Catholic high school, I'm the only one who has buried a parent and nobody, including myself, is exactly sure how to deal with this fact. Silence seems to be the acceptable solution.

Every year the school has a father-daughter dance. It's a fund-raising event to help pay for the extra supplies the school needs. The students pick a theme, decorate the gym, and solicit raffle donations from local businesses. There are committees for everything from setup to cleanup, and all students are urged to participate.

"I know how difficult this is for you, Jacquelyn," Sister Patricia says when she catches me gazing at a poster advertising the premier school event of 1967. "But life moves forward. In time you will be able to talk about your dad and smile."

She's wrong! I cry myself to sleep every night, and I avoid the movie theater where Dad and I used to attend the cowboy extravaganza marathon every month. I worry constantly, too, but not about passing world history. I fear I will forget the sound of my father's voice.

"Your father is gone, and you must make a life without him," Sister Patricia says as she points to the sign-up sheets tacked to the bulletin board beside the poster. "Start by helping out with some aspect of the dance. Sell raffle tickets or serve the lemonade."

I don't want a life without him! Why is this so hard for others to understand? I want my dad here with me now! We had plans, things we would do together. . .things that now will never be done.

Friday night I'm in my pajamas by 6:00. If I can force myself to sleep, I won't think about the dance. Then, on Monday, maybe I'll come down with some disease that will keep me out of school until the after-event talk becomes old news.

Suddenly I hear our apartment doorbell ring, then the sound of

my Uncle Edmund's voice.
Edmund is my father's
brother, a bachelor by
choice. Usually he stops by
every Sunday afternoon for
a visit, but today isn't
Sunday. Is something
wrong? Filled with curiosity,
I venture from my bedroom to investigate.

Uncle Edmund is dressed in his best black suit. At
the sight of me, he smiles and remarks, "I hope you
aren't planning to wear pajamas to the school dance.
I believe something fancier is required."

All color drains from my face, and my throat
tightens. I look to my mother for help, for her to tell
Uncle Edmund I can't go to the dance with him. Yes,
he's a wonderful uncle, and I love him, but this dance
is for fathers and their daughters.

"I figured you'd forget to buy the tickets, so I
stopped by the school and picked them up." Uncle
Edmund smiles at me. "I sneaked a peek at the gym,
too. It looks great with all the flowers, rainbows, and
stars. What's this year's theme?"

"Feeling Groovy." My mouth is as dry as cotton. Why didn't the clergymember who sold Uncle Edmund the tickets tell him what this dance is all about? "But I can't...."

"You're right," Uncle Edmund interrupts. "You can't begin to get ready until I give you the other ticket." From his front jacket pocket he takes out a small orange ticket, identical to the ones used at the movie theater. He hands it to me with the instruction, "Read what's written on the back."

I turn the ticket over, instantly recognizing my father's handwriting. On this ticket my father wrote: "Good for one father event."

"Your father fought very hard to live, but when he realized he couldn't win the battle, he turned his attention to your future," Uncle Edmund softly explains. "He filled out more than a hundred such tickets and gave them to me to hold. I promised him I'd make sure you did

with me all you had planned to do with him. That includes this dance. I spoke to your school principal, and she agrees with the validity of this ticket. Substitute dads are acceptable escorts."

Tears blind me. I can't move or think. Even though my dad is no longer here, he is still taking good care of me.

Reaching out, my uncle uses a fingertip to wipe away my tears. "Hurry now. You get ready while I go pick up your corsage. Your mother says the dress you wore to Vincent's wedding is perfect for tonight." He clicks his heels together. "We don't want to miss the dance contest. I do a mean tango."

Uncle Edmund and I attend the father-daughter dance that night, and in the years that follow we use tickets stating things such as "Good for one Broadway show," "Good for one prom dress shopping spree," and "Good for one high school graduation dinner." Eventually Uncle Edmund learns to like Roy Rogers movies; I learn to tango. In time, as Sister Patricia predicted, I could even talk about my dad and smile.

I don't think any child ever gets over the death of a parent. However, I consider myself lucky that my father loved me so much he unselfishly helped his only brother to become my hero. Because of Uncle Edmund, I was able to do many of the things my dad and I had planned to do. And even though Dad wasn't actually there with me, he has always been there in my heart.

*In a moment of quiet, dark stillness,*
*or even in the bustle of daily life,*
*you may occasionally feel that*
*you are in the company of an angel.*
*Revel in its divine presence!*

# Fishing with Granny

M Y BROTHER AND I called her Granny even though she wasn't really our grandmother. She lived in southern Georgia where the land is flat, Spanish moss swings lazily from trees, and the gnats swarm in black, static clouds during the sluggish summers. Her old house had a tin roof; when it rained, the patter of raindrops could lull almost anyone into a sound sleep.

In that house, Granny had raised seven children by herself; my stepfather was the youngest. I had always felt like an outsider—even in my own home— after my mother married him. I just didn't seem to fit in with everyone else.

I remember Granny best during the summer because that's when we usually visited. One summer, I spent a week alone with her, without my mom and stepdad. Every morning started with Granny cooking eggs and frying up sausage and bacon from her neighbor's farm. My mouth would water for her homemade biscuits. I always poked holes in them to fill with sweet syrup. After breakfast, Granny washed the dishes in a porcelain pan in the sink, letting them dry on a drain board. Then she would wash clothes using the old wringer-washer on the back porch. After the clothes came through the wringer, I would help her hang them outside to dry.

When her other grandchildren stopped by—and they always did—she would make time for them. She asked what they were up to and listened to their problems. I noticed how special she made them feel, but no matter how hard I tried to feel like a part of Granny's family, I still felt left out.

One day, Granny took me on a long walk past her garden to the pond in back. She sat down on a moss-covered rock while I fished. My brother and I always enjoyed fishing together, so I figured I'd give it a shot without him. I wasn't a wimp—I baited my own hook—but I could never get the fish off the hook without being finned. I tried to be brave, but I could not stand being finned. When I reeled in my first fish that day, I left it flipping and flopping on the bank.

"Aren't you going to get that fish off the hook?" Granny asked.

"I will," I told her. "As soon as the fish dies."

Granny ignored me. Reaching down and grasping that fish nice and easy, she pulled the hook out. "Next time, you do it," she said, putting the fish in a bucket.

It took awhile, but I finally got the hang of taking the fish off the hook. Though I was grateful for her help, I thought she felt obligated to help me. I figured she had to be nice to me because her son was married to my mom.

When my little sister was born, Granny put together a quilt for her baby bed. I remember thinking, "Of course she made a quilt for her. My sister is her own flesh and blood."

It wasn't until Christmas that I finally realized she didn't make a distinction between any of the grandchildren. That year, she gave all of her grandkids a gift. The girls were each given a super-stuffed red stocking with gold tassels, and the boys received their gifts wrapped in bright red Christmas paper tied up with a gold bow. A gold-painted pinecone was taped to each box.

I sat in a corner munching some candy, knowing that I wouldn't get as much as the "real" grandkids. When I looked inside my stocking, I found a pair of socks, a box of crayons, and a handful of pencils with my name on them—the same gifts she gave the other children. But then I noticed another package—one with a red bow and a package of gummy worms taped to it. I eagerly ripped it open to see a small fishing tackle box with plastic worms and hooks in it. I smiled, thinking of my previous fear of getting finned by a fish, and when I turned to thank Granny, she winked at me. I knew then that I was, and always had been, a part of her family.

# A Final Good-bye

URING THE SUMMER of his twentieth year, Bill, my handsome brother, suddenly died. I was out of school for the season, just turning 12, and full of youth. I was happy we were staying with Bill's fiancée, Ivy, waiting for the wedding that would coincide with his twenty-first birthday.

The house was aglow with preparations. The smell of food made my mouth water, and I got a quick tap on the wrist when I tried to sneak a huge piece of cake off the table. The place buzzed with laughter and high excitement.

I was being fitted in my lavender dress, standing on a stool, trying to be patient. Smiling, my brother came in, put his arm around my shoulders, and said to me, "You'll be a lovely bridesmaid." His deep blue eyes sparkled with love, and I hugged him hard.

The days of the week passed happily until that Friday morning when I slipped into Bill's bedroom intending to surprise him. But my brother lay still and white-faced, and when I touched his cheek, it was cold and clammy.

Scared, I tumbled down the stairs, running into Ivy's mother as she came out of the kitchen. "What's wrong?" she asked, holding my arms. "It's Bill. I can't wake him," I cried, tears running down my cheeks. Her face showed concern as she hurried to check on him, knocking on the bedroom door and pushing me backward. "Go get Ivy, please."

An ambulance arrived, its sirens blasting through the still morning air. I watched two men carry my brother out on a white stretcher from the house, a worried Ivy climbing into the ambulance with him. A cluster of neighbors stood on their doorsteps, faces grim, arms folded.

The home that had been so full of celebration now lay quiet and still for two days. Everyone acted as if silence was a necessary thing.

"We have to wait and see," said Ivy's mother to my inquiries. "Bill is in critical condition. The doctor says it's his heart." I knew he'd had rheumatic fever several times.

"Can I go to the hospital?" I asked. For a moment she stood still and thought, drying her hands on a dish towel. "Not right now," she said finally, brushing my hair from my face. "Ivy's with him. Just say a prayer for him. Will you do that?"

Our parents had both died a few years earlier. All Bill and I had was each other, and I must have sent a hundred prayers to heaven while we all waited in that somber house for news.

When Ivy returned alone on the third day, I knew by the despair on her lovely young face that the worst had happened. "He died at 11:00 this morning," she sobbed and wrapped her arms around me, holding me as if I were the most precious thing in the world.

Bill was buried on a hot August afternoon that smelled of flowers, green grass, and summertime. The sky was a cloudless blue, and his coffin was covered with so many wreaths, the scent of carnations filled the air around us. I felt lost among so many grown-up mourners, even shivering in the sunshine, feeling as desperately alone as only a 12-year-old can.

Summer came to an end. The wedding gifts were returned one by one, and I went back to school carrying my sorrow deep in my heart. The adults didn't notice that I'd never had a chance to say good-bye to my brother.

Soon it was February, and winter was bearing down with an icy fist. Snow began to fall heavily as I left my piano teacher's home after my weekly lesson. I walked there and back every Saturday, about a mile. As the snow thickened, I decided to cut through the large nearby woods where big trees grew close together, heading in the direction of school. I barely noticed that daylight was slipping away from me. An hour went by, and the storm deepened. I became uneasy at making no headway. Now I could barely lift one foot after the other.

Where was I? Endless snowscapes blew into high drifts, leaving me no landmarks. Stopping suddenly in the middle of a terrible white world, I realized I was lost, alone, and beginning to shiver with the encroaching cold of night.

In that forlorn moment of silence, I felt something come over me. My shivering stopped, and I began moving, as if I knew where to go. Even more curious, I started to think I could smell carnations. But how could that be?

I felt no fear, only amazement as I walked gingerly through the worst winter blizzard to hit the area in a dozen years. Then I saw bright lights blazing in the distance, and I called out in relief.

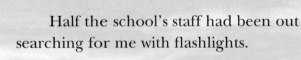

Half the school's staff had been out searching for me with flashlights.

"Hello! Here I am!" At that precise moment, the fragrant scent of flowers disappeared. My companion was gone. I smiled and whispered, "Good-bye, Bill, and thank you."

Back at school, standing in the doorway, my friends cheered and slapped my back. I stamped the snow from my shoes and smiled as my teacher handed me a blanket and a cup of hot chocolate. "My goodness! You smell just like flowers. Are you wearing perfume?"

"I'm safe! I'm really safe!" I exclaimed to myself.

Stepping into the cheery warmth of the room, I shrugged off my snow-covered coat and stretched my cold hands toward the fire blazing in the hearth, grateful for the heat. I never told anyone what had happened. As young as I was, I didn't think they'd believe me—or that anyone else would as I grew older. So I kept it to myself, until now.

Whenever a high wind rattles my windowpanes and winter snow settles upon the earth, I think back to that night. I have to conclude that from wherever sweet souls go, my young brother—gone too soon—was allowed to return to lead me through a snowstorm and say a final good-bye at last.

Companion, confidante, buddy, and pal,
perpetual miracle sent from above.
I thank God each day for the gift of an angel,
beautiful blessing of friendship and love.

Angels reflect the magnificence of heaven—
the spectacular home God has prepared
for all those who belong to him.

# A Message from Popsy

"He was my hero and my cheerleader, my support in times of doubt and lack of faith. He was my hope when all seemed hopeless, my reason to keep on trying. He was my best friend, my grandfather, my dear guardian angel."

Marnie's voice choked with grief as she read the words she had written just for her Popsy. Now at his eulogy, she missed him more than ever and wondered whether she would ever be able to make her dreams come true without him.

From the time she had first dared to dream of becoming a novelist, her Popsy had been there to cheer her on even when her own parents had constantly urged her to "think about something a little more secure" for a career choice. It was all she ever heard, but Popsy had always laughed off all that well-meaning advice with his own brand of wisdom.

"Go for what you want, Marnie. You've only one life, so live it the way you see fit. Remember, you are a child of the universe, no less than the trees and the stars; you have a right to be here. Shine, child, shine!"

Marnie could always count on Popsy to lift her spirits as she began her writing career, collecting rejection slips and courting failure with her first miserable attempt at a novel. It was Popsy who forced her to find another agent's address, package another query and proposal, and send out another copy of her manuscript. And she did time and time again. Then suddenly the form letter rejections became personal notes of encouragement from agents eager to see her work once it matured and revised.

Marnie would show Popsy these letters when Marnie and her folks visited, which had become more frequent just as he was becoming weaker with age.

"See, this is proof you are on the path God set out for you, Marnie. Remember, you are a child of the universe, no less than the trees and the stars; you have a right to be here. And whether or not it is clear to you, no doubt the universe is unfolding just as it should, so don't ever give up!"

On that fateful day her mother called her with the news, Marnie found herself at a complete loss for words for the first time in her life. Without warning, like a thief in the night, her beloved Popsy had been stolen from her. The autopsy would show massive heart failure. He had died in his sleep, and now she felt as though her dreams were dead, too.

For the funeral, Marnie's grandmother Jeanne had asked her to write and read something special. It was the first time anyone in Marnie's family, other than Popsy, had ever acknowledged her writing talent. Ironic that it came at such a heartbreaking time. But Marnie said she would be honored, and she stood on trembling legs and read through a shaking voice a three-page tribute to her Popsy, breaking down in tears at the end.

Now she was in a permanent free fall. Her ambitions and dreams drifted further away from her while she continued to fall toward the ground. Marnie felt as though she was about to crash and the darkness of despair was ready to swallow her whole.

It was then that Marnie's grandmother handed her a large box. There were tears in her eyes. "Popsy wanted to be sure you got this, honey," she said. Marnie looked into the box and touched the books. "He knew how much you loved books. These were his all-time favorites."

As Marnie picked up the books and looked through them, she could almost feel Popsy right there, telling her how much he loved her writing style and how successful she would one day be. "Your name will be on tons of these one day, you'll see," he would say. The way Marnie now felt, she didn't think that would ever happen, especially now that her only support system was gone from her life.

Just then, a large laminated bookmark fell out from one of the books and onto the floor. Marnie bent over and picked it up. On the colorful bookmark was a long quote called "Desiderata" by somebody named Max Ehrmann. Marnie read through it and came to several underscored lines.

The lines read, "You are a child of the universe, no less than the trees and the stars; you have a right to be here. And whether or not it is clear to you, no doubt the universe is unfolding just as it should."

Through tear-filled eyes, Marnie read and re-read those lines. She could almost hear his voice and feel his comforting arms about her. Then something made her turn the bookmark over. On the back, her Popsy had scrawled, "For my Marnie. Shine, child, shine!"

All the doubt, the fear, and the lack of faith seemed to vanish from Marnie's mind and heart and soul when she read those words. Never again did she look back.

Nine months later, she secured an agent and signed a two-book deal with a major publishing company. And on her first published novel's dedication page, she wrote "For my Popsy, who taught me how to shine."

*If you've looked to the stars at night to find an angel chorus, you've done well. If you've looked into your heart to find the angel's song, you've done better.*

# My Angelic Daughter

MAYA WAS NAMED after my favorite author and poet, Maya Angelou. Like her namesake, my daughter is wise—more wise than her six years. With a gap where her four front teeth should be and eyes that sparkle like the Fourth of July, she is a tiny, doll-like darling. Throughout her young life, Maya has suffered from many health problems, so she is smaller than most girls her age. This makes her self-conscious, but also more sensitive to others' feelings.

Last year, Maya was in kindergarten. One day she came home from school, bubbling over with excitement. "Mama, guess what!" she shouted, nearly breathless as she bounced through the front door. "There's a new girl in my class and she doesn't speak any English and I'm her new best friend! I decided today!" she proclaimed jubilantly.

"Honey, slow down," I told her, laughing at her exuberance. Maya does and says everything with exuberance. Eventually, she calmed down enough to tell me about a new girl from Mexico, who had joined her class that day. Her name was Isabel, and that was the extent of her English: her name.

So Maya took it upon herself to become her best friend. It never occurred to her that Isabel's Spanish and Maya's English might be a problem. To a six-year-old, communication is taken for granted. All Maya cared about was that this new little girl had cried all day and had no one to talk to.

When it came time for the class Halloween party, I met Isabel. She clung to Maya, clearly scared and avoiding contact with anyone else. Never smiling, she sat as the other kids played games, only watching the laughter and the fun, never attempting to join in. Her teacher later told me that Maya was the only one

Isabel would sit with at lunch or play with at recess. She was afraid to speak and never participated in class. The really amazing thing was that Maya didn't know a word of Spanish. As a teacher of the hearing impaired, I was impressed by their nonverbal communication skills.

The days flew by, and each day Maya came home from school babbling about her day, how it went, what Isabel learned, and so on. I was happy for her and her new friend, but I didn't really think much of it. Then one day Maya's teacher called to ask if I would teach sign language for the year-end kindergarten program. She also told me what a wonderful child Maya was and what a good friend. I was pleased, but the impact of what she was saying didn't sink in until I went to her class to teach.

I still remembered Isabel from the Halloween party several months before. But that shy, withdrawn, paralyzed-with-fear little girl was now a radiant, confident, happy child. Her big brown eyes were as sparkly as Maya's. And she smiled! I could hardly believe the transformation! She still spoke very little English, but now she tried to participate in class. As the teacher and I talked, I watched Maya and Isabel play together. Most of their communication consisted of pointing, helping, gesturing. And smiling.

Maya would look into her little friend's eyes and smile the sweetest, widest smile I had ever seen. It was enough to melt your heart. And Isabel would smile right back at her with a shy, priceless smile. Her teacher told me of the gradual transformation that had taken place. She told me how day after day, Maya would sacrifice her free time to sit patiently with her scared little friend, often defending her to the other kids, always being kind, and never, ever giving up on Isabel. My eyes filled with tears as she described my tiny little girl's tremendous heart and selflessness.

When Maya and I were alone that night, I told her how proud I was of her, how she was a true friend. I admitted that I could learn a thing or two from her beautiful example of friendship. Then I asked her how she did it—how she created this amazing friendship without a word of language. My blue-eyed angel looked up at me and said simply, "I smiled."

She told me how every time Isabel would cry or look sad, she would just do her best to reassure her with a smile, sticking close to her, always letting her know that she had a friend.

Maya and Isabel had first-grade class together this year, and next year they'll be in the same class for second grade. Every time I see Isabel, I remember the scared little girl she once was and how my little daughter was her true friend. Maya is my hero and my greatest reason to smile.

*Angels give themselves fully,*
*for they have seen the face of love.*

# *Every Day Is a Good Day*

IT WAS JUNE 21, 1987, when my son, John Quinn, woke up with a pain in his groin. I assumed it was a pulled muscle or hernia since he was a BMX bicycle racer. He was 13 years old and, after being involved in racing for only three years, already had many first-place trophies. Concerned but not frightened about his pain, we headed for the emergency room.

After arriving at the ER, John was examined and blood work was done. I heard the doctors say, "Something is wrong—the blood clotted before we could get it to the lab." I had a sinking feeling and knew in my heart this would be serious. I was told that John would have to be admitted because they thought he might have leukemia. I felt as if I was having a bad dream. In shock, I phoned my husband and daughter and told them to come to the hospital.

In the meantime, the nurses were joking with John—he was being his usual jovial self, unaware of what was going on. My husband and daughter arrived shortly. We were told John's white count was 550,000; the normal range is between 4,000 and 10,000. He could have died instantly from a stroke. The nurses told me to go home and pack a bag because John needed to go to Children's Hospital of Philadelphia (CHOP). We drove home, but all I can remember about the ride was screaming and thinking that this couldn't be happening.

We returned to the hospital in what felt like a matter of minutes, and then we followed the ambulance for the 65-mile ride. All sorts of things went through my mind. I had always prayed for my children, but now my prayers were more intense than ever.

After our arrival at CHOP, we were led to John's room on the cancer floor.

We saw sick young children everywhere, some bald, some vomiting into buckets. Soon John's diagnosis was confirmed: leukemia. They took us into a room and told us the form he had was chronic and not a child's form, but the adult form, which was very rare in children. They gave him two years to live. My husband and I cried hysterically. Then the doctors asked us to tell John. How do you tell a 13-year-old he has two years to live? We all cried together.

I stayed with John at the hospital. Many tests were run, and the doctors managed to get his white count down. We were told the only chance for a cure was a bone marrow transplant.

After 11 days, we came home. John was on chemo pills to keep his white count under control. He didn't lose his hair, so he never looked sick, but he felt awful those first few weeks. We returned to Philadelphia every week for blood counts.

Even through all of the pills and tests and driving and sickness, John amazed me with his positive attitude. It never seemed to occur to him to let this sickness beat him. He wanted to continue racing, which he did, going on to win more trophies.

In September 1988, the bone marrow transplant was arranged. John's donor was his sister. Though she wasn't a perfect match, she was anxious to help her brother. We found a doctor in Iowa who specialized in mismatch transplants. Dr. Trigg was very knowledgeable and could answer any question I threw at him. John really liked him, and I did, too.

The transplant was done, and John never complained about any of it. His courage and bravery throughout the ordeal set an example for the rest of us. We stayed in Iowa for three months and then returned home.

John was cancer-free for one year, during which time he was tutored at home. We were sure this operation had cured him and he would soon be able to get on with his life, but then we got the call: The leukemia was back.

All I kept thinking was that my son would not get to go to the prom, learn how to drive,

graduate from high school, or
get married. He would miss out
on so much, and there would
be an irreparable hole where
John had once been in our
lives. I knew the situation was
out of my control, and all I
could do was pray. I asked God
that my son might have a long
and happy life.

John continued living each day to its fullest. He
never wanted people to know of his illness or give him
sympathy. His motto was "Every day above ground is a
good day." He went on racing until he was 16, learned
to drive, finished high school with his class, went on to
computer tech school, and finished that, too. And, yes,
he went to the prom and had a girlfriend. He also had
some wonderful friends, and he was always there to
lend them a hand if they needed it. After he ended his
BMX career, he started racing 4-wheelers and fixing
motorcycles. He'd buy ones that needed a lot of work,
fix them up, and sell them. He eventually made
enough money to buy the sports car of his dreams.

John amazed his doctors. He lived on his chemo pills for years. He was tired a lot and had terrible mouth sores from the pills, but that did not stop him from doing whatever he wanted to do. He and I seldom spoke of his illness, though he once told me he was not afraid to die, but he was worried because he knew I would be devastated. I always told him I would do everything in my power to help him.

In March 1996, he got a job fixing motorcycles. He was so happy and loved what he was doing. Then one day I got a call that his blood work had shown blast cells. We knew what that meant. John came home from work smiling as usual, and then he saw the look on our faces. It almost killed me to tell him the news. Once again I had to be strong and convince him there was still hope. We went to his local doctors, and they gave us grim news: John had six weeks to live. The one slim option was a stem cell transplant. John was a little reluctant, but since it seemed to be the only hope, he agreed to have the operation.

I wanted him to go to Dr. Trigg in Iowa, but there wasn't enough time. So we went to the University of Pennsylvania, and John underwent the procedure there. I lived in his room for six weeks, and I prayed almost constantly. Two weeks into his transplant John became very ill and was moved to the ICU. By this time his heart had been damaged by the drugs. I would watch his face and see expressions that looked to me like he was carrying on a conversation with someone. After two weeks in the ICU, he was brought back to his room. For a while, he could not talk because his vocal cords were paralyzed.

He eventually came home, and a nurse came by every day to administer IV antibiotics. John ran fevers of 105° for four months. I watched my 150-pound son drop to 110 pounds. He asked me why God didn't just take him. He told me to put his ashes on the mantel.

On September 8, 1996, he turned 23, and on September 28, John Quinn passed away. We held his hands until the end.

The memorial service consisted of 400 people from all walks of life. John had told me he was afraid no one would remember him except me, but I'm sure he knows now how many people loved him. Even his doctor cried at his service.

John was such an inspiration to all of us—he always lit up a room just by entering it. Even though he was robbed of his childhood, he never felt sorry for himself. He was a boy, but he had the maturity of a man. He lived nine years with his cross, and he died like a hero. I'm so proud to be his mother.

We've endured more than six years without him now, and the worst part is not being able to hug him. The pain in my heart remains, but John's spirit lives on. Dr. Trigg adopted a little boy and named him Quinn. Two of John's friends had babies and also named them Quinn. We will never forget him. I had always feared death before, but my son taught me not to be afraid. Not only did he teach me how to die, but he also taught me how to live.

# More Than a Stepdad

BY THE TIME I turned 14 last year, I guess you could say I'd learned a lot about life and weird situations. And about angels. But that came much later.

I was just seven when I had to learn my first hard lesson about life. My dad got really sick that year. He had to have surgery a bunch of times and really hated the fact that my mom, Tammy, had to support us. I think it was one of those "male dominant trait" things. I was too young to understand why it finally got so bad that, as he kept getting sicker, he reached the point of no return and took his own life. As if a seven-year-old could under-stand any of it, which I didn't. I only knew that I missed him a lot. So did my older sister, Bethany, and brother, Bobby. What I understood most was that my mom was really sad.

I had happy memories of the years before my dad got sick and knew that he and my mom had been really happy. I guess that explains why I understood and wasn't upset when she met Kenneth and fell in love again. I wanted her to be happy, and he seemed like a nice man. The whole family thought he could be the answer to our problems and be a loving fatherly figure, which we kids all wanted and needed.

We were wrong.

It went OK at first. He treated us really well, but then after the wedding he changed. He didn't have too much to do with me...maybe because I was the "spittin' image" of my dad. Or maybe he just didn't care. I still don't know. Finally, my brother moved out, and my mother decided she just couldn't take it anymore.

There was a very long, problem-filled divorce, mainly about who got possession of the house we were building. We had

to move away, but after some details got worked out, we got to move back home. That whole situation was another really hard lesson. Luckily, I got to stay in the same school during the moves, which made it easier.

It didn't take school, though, to teach me that guys are a lot of trouble...probably more than they're worth, I had decided by my fourteenth birthday. But then I saw how lonely my mom was, and I realized she would soon be really alone. My brother was married and already gone, and my sister would be out of school and leaving soon, too. And I'd been planning to go to college and become a journalist and writer once I was done with high school.

"Dear God," I prayed every day, "please send someone who will make my mother happy." But if that was going to happen, I decided, my mom had to do her part.

"You need to be dating," I told her one day. "You gotta get out of this house." I don't know who was more surprised by what I said, she or I. "You'll be OK," I assured her when she hesitated.

Believe me, though, she dated some guys who made me wonder what was wrong with me for ever suggesting the idea to her. But I kept praying, and one day she brought home someone different. His name was James Newcomb. The fact that he was so different actually scared me.

*Whoa,* I thought. *She's going to get hurt. Again.*

I tried talking to her. "I don't want you being with him," I insisted. "I've changed my mind about you going out."

"Give him a chance," my mother said.

*Why should I?* I asked myself. *If you risk loving someone, you just wind up getting hurt.* But I did as she asked. Soon, my mother was beginning to smile. There was a twinkle in her eye. She was in love with James and he with her. I saw how happy he made her...opening her heart up to love. Oh, how he treated her! He did lots of little things...sentimental and personal things. If she said she liked something, he would get her a card or small gift that was a reminder of it. It told me he was truly paying attention. Most of all, though, he listened to her. And, surprise of all surprises, he even listened to me.

Not being listened to—or noticed—is the loneliest thing in the world. But James cared about me and what I felt and thought. He gave me a chance to speak my mind about everything and treated me as he did his own three children. It didn't take me long to figure out his love limits...there weren't any. He had enough love and kindness for all of us, and he didn't try to take my mother out of my life, either.

"Come with me to pick out your mother's ring," he invited me. "You know what she likes." No one was happier at a wedding than I was at theirs.

I will always think of James as my father, no "step" about it. We spend a lot of time together...sharing birthday parties, bike rides, picnics, and ball games. Our daily life is wonderful, as only life can be when guided by an angel. Oh yes, James is an angel. What else could he be?

I have always believed in angels. It makes sense, really, when you think about it. God needs someone to help us out. If you are like me, though, your first thought when you hear "angels" is creatures with golden halos, long white silken robes tied with belts of sunflowers, wings that sparkle in the sunlight, and beauty that can put a smile on even the saddest face.

But this angel, James, has black hair, a beard, and a mustache. He laughs a lot and likes to drive his new Camaro. He hides Christmas gifts (a sapphire ring for me) in Cracker Jack boxes. He always listens and— even more important—remembers what I say.  If I talk about something that's important to me, he'll bring it up again weeks later…and he always shows that he cares about my opinions, feelings, and ideas. From the first day he walked into my life, he's made it better for me and my family. I thank God for him every day.

James has more than earned his angel wings, for he had a really tough job: gaining the love and affection of someone who's always been deathly scared of trusting another person. Now I'm not. Who else but one of God's marvelous angels could make such a change happen?

# Grandma Mary

GRANDMA MARY WAS my guardian angel. She had to be. That's what I decided when I was ten years old during the short time she was in my life. And that's what I still believe to this day—35 years later. She came from nowhere when I truly needed her and returned to heaven not long after her work was done.

Before Mary, I never remember my grandfather dating anyone. He was a gregarious man who lived alone in his beautiful old apartment and never seemed lonely. He had a full and active life. Popie owned a clothing store, which employed our entire family, and was extremely active both in our small town and in our religious community. He usually ate dinner with my mother and me, and the three of us always had a great time. We didn't need anyone else to join the family. We were just fine.

Then one weekend we were taken by surprise when he introduced us to his new "lady friend." Her name was Mary, and she lived in a neighboring town. All I knew was that a friend of my grandfather's had introduced them several weeks prior to our meeting. Mary was delightful. She appeared to me to have stepped right out of a storybook in the role of "grandmother." She was a short lady—plump and friendly. She always wore little suits with the skirt pulled up beneath her bosom and the open jacket never closing over her round  tummy. They were married shortly after, and Mary immediately became "Grandma Mary" and my favorite person in the universe.

Within several weeks of the wedding, my mother was injured unexpectedly and required extensive hospitalization. I was frightened and certain she would die and that I would end up all alone. Mary immediately stepped forward and insisted that I move in with my "grandma" and grandpa. I didn't realize until later what this would've meant to a new wife in a new town suddenly saddled with a ten-year-old child for an open-ended amount of time. Yet, she didn't seem to be concerned with anything except providing a loving home for me.

My life took on a storybook quality of its own. Living with Mary was like being wrapped in a cocoon of special love and warmth unlike anything I had ever known before. Because she and my grandpa lived too far from my school for me to walk home for lunch, Mary would pick me up outside school every day and take me for my favorite meal—a hamburger and french fries. She did this EVERY day! She was tuned in to everything that I liked and disliked in life. I was an extremely shy and quiet child, so this was quite an accomplishment and continuously astonished and delighted me.

Of course, there were difficult moments. I missed my mother very much and was worried that she would  die. Because of Mary, what I recall most about that year was not the sadness and fear but her warmth and love. Every night after dinner, she insisted that the three of us play cards or other games. We always laughed and hugged, and one day I won a big shiny box of pennies, which I have kept to this day. As I look back now, it was as though I had fallen into a Norman Rockwell painting where everything was peaceful and perfect.

I often picture my grandma standing in the kitchen with the little suit jacket off and an apron perched precariously on that plump tummy. One day I walked in and caught her in the act of something that I simply could not believe. She stood at the counter with the trash bag close at hand. She had purchased my favorite brand of cupcakes and was actually throwing away the cake because she knew my very favorite part was the frosting! That memory will forever bring a smile to my face and a tear to my eye.

After a year, my mother was sufficiently recovered from her back surgery to take care of me once again. I rather reluctantly went home and found myself missing Mary and the life I had come to know with her. It was several months after I had moved back home that

Mary suddenly had to be hospitalized. "Nothing serious," everyone said. We didn't even make the trip out of town to see her. I was assured that she would be back home in a few days.

That Sunday night the phone rang. We were having dinner with my extended family when my mother picked up the phone. It was Mary. My mother spoke briefly and explained that we were eating. Instead of finishing the call or offering to call back later when the family had gone, Mary uncharacteristically insisted that we pass the phone around to every single one of us. That night, she spoke for a few minutes with every member of the family. I got to talk with her, too. We didn't realize until later how odd that was for her to insist that she speak to everyone.

We went home, and all was quiet until the middle of the night. There was a knock. My mother gathered her robe around her and padded down the stairs. My cousin had come—she had urgent news. I crept to the top of the stairs, and I knew before anyone spoke, before I could hear the crying from the kitchen, before my mother called me to come downstairs. I simply and absolutely KNEW that my Grandma Mary had died.

That night I cried myself to sleep while praying that when I woke up I would find that it had all been just a terrible nightmare. But Mary was gone. Just as quickly as she had come into our lives, she had slipped out.

My mother fully recovered, and I never needed to stay with anyone else again. My grandfather slowly got over his grief and married for a third time. The poor woman never had a chance. She could never be my grandma. No. My grandma had been an angel—a plump little angel with a ready smile and a hug that could comfort any hurt—an angel who took me under her wing and filled my tummy with treats and my heart with love.

I remain convinced to this day that Grandma Mary was—and still is—my guardian angel. Only now her job is tougher, as she not only has to look after me—but my daughter, too. We talk about Mary often, and Danya knows that Mary is watching over her. She also knows that sometimes it's OK to throw away the cake and just eat the frosting.

*If angels had a job description,*
*it would only consist of one task:*
*Do the work of love.*

*Angels have visited humanity by streams and*
*in deserts, by cradles and by graves,*
*by altars and by bedsides. Angels have touched us*
*at the holiest and earthiest of places,*
*but they have seldom left us the*
*same way they found us.*

# My Own Precious Angel

*I* MUST ADMIT THERE was a time when I had little or no faith in a higher power. I grew up poor in a family of five. My father was a drug addict who molested me. I watched our lives go downhill as my eldest brother and father spent most of their time in jail for various reasons. Growing up in such an environment, I had no hope for happiness. Yet, oddly enough, I always dreamed that someday I would go to college. My mother encouraged me in this, and I worked hard to get good grades. I tried to stay out of trouble, and that usually meant staying away from my family. I threw myself into school and community activities. But at the end of the day, when I went back home, the reality of our lives always hit me hard.

It was doubtful that I'd ever really go to college. In high school I managed to line up some financial aid, along with a few small scholarships, but together they were not nearly enough. I wanted to go so badly, but I refused to consider our local community college because I knew I needed to get as far away as possible from the negative influences of home. Finally, the day before I had to register, my mother pawned her jewelry so that I could go.

In 1995, I went across the country to go to college. I had envisioned college as my escape, my salvation, but to my bewilderment, the poverty, loneliness, and negativity of my background followed me there. Violence, the news of more incarcerations, and my mother's desperation as she turned to me for comfort spilled into my world over the phone lines. I felt overwhelming guilt that I had left when she obviously needed me at home. I had gone away, yes, but I had not escaped.

So instead of rejoicing at my new life, I became trapped in a whirlwind of depression. The view I most often saw was the ground. I made no eye contact with anyone, and I spent most of my time sleeping. I often caught myself hoping that God would just take my life.

I even found myself considering that maybe I should just give up, stop trying to do things the "right way." What was the point of trying so hard when you could look around and see a criminal doing better than you were? The age-old dilemma became mine: Good or bad, which way should I go?

One day, an angel tried to talk to me in the school cafeteria, only I didn't know yet that he was an angel. I barely gave him so much as a glance. He sat down and called me by name. Startled, I looked up to see an average guy smiling at me.

It turned out he was in one of my classes, and later that day he spoke to me again. There was no escaping him. He invited me to go walking with him that night, and I'm not sure why, but I said yes. I was very distrustful and suspicious of people, especially men. But as I came to know him, he began to open my eyes. He talked to me about things I had never thought of. He showed me aspects of the world and the heavens I had never considered.

One night while we were out walking, he told me to extend my arms and close my eyes. Then he asked, "Do you know what it feels like to be an angel?" He assured me that angels come in many different forms. Until then, I'd never thought about angels or religion, but after that we would sometimes sit together and look into the sky while he told me about God.

As the months passed, I found myself falling in love with this angel. He cared for me and taught me to walk tall. He told me to "always make a future and not a past." He promised to stay with me through all of time and proved his commitment by marrying me.

We were happy together, but not without troubles. Soon, I was pregnant and too ill to continue with college or even to work part-time. Because of my illness, my husband also had to leave school, and he worked three jobs to support us. He told me not to worry, that he had plenty of time to finish his degree.

Despite all his efforts, we could not afford furniture, and many times the utilities were cut off. For seven months of my pregnancy I slept on a cold floor wrapped in extra clothing. My angel did all that he could. He even began selling his blood for extra cash. Just like Jesus, he gave his blood to save me. At the time, however, I didn't appreciate it. Things were rough, and I resented the way we were living. One day I went into a rage and began throwing around the little bit of property we did have. My angel stopped me and brought me to my knees. He said, "Right here, right now—let's put all differences aside and pray." At that moment, God did what I had asked him to do many years before: He took my life.

That's when everything changed. We joined a church and began to pray as a family. My husband got one good job that paid all the bills. Our baby was born healthy, despite a lack of nutritious food during my pregnancy. We eventually moved to a larger place and filled our home with furniture.

The city where we lived ran an annual contest that highlighted families who'd struggled to overcome adversity, and from these they selected one to be Family of the Year. I knew of many worthy families and offered to help our church write some nominations. To my surprise, they encouraged me to tell our story. At the last minute I did, and no one was more shocked than I was when we were named Family of the Year. Because of all the publicity, the CEO of the corporation where my husband worked was inspired to give us $5,000 and to provide my husband with a salaried position.

Since then, life has been fairly smooth. Don't get me wrong—we've had ups and downs. For example, both my son and I recently became ill and were hospitalized. At one point, my son had a prolonged fever seizure, and we thought he would not make it. But we prayed over him, and soon he was as beautiful and healthy as ever. After that, God let us know that he was with us because every morning for a week a rainbow shone across the wall in our bedroom.

I've learned that God presents us with tests, and when we pass he shows us exactly how he feels. It's his way of making sure that we're still faithful. It's almost as if, while we are saying thank you to God, God is saying thank you to us for not losing the faith.

I realize now that angels really do come in all forms. My husband is a true angel sent by God to save me from destruction. When I was faced with the choice between good and evil, my angel stopped me from making the wrong decision. It's no wonder then that whenever I look at his face I remember why every night I say a prayer, thanking God for my own precious angel.

*If you pray truly, you will feel within yourself a great assurance, and the angels will be your companions.*

Evagrius of Pontus, *Search of the Spirit*